WITH CHRIST AT SEA

With Christ at Sea

a Religious Autobiography

By Frank T. Bullen Author of

'The Cruise of the Cachalot,' etc.

LONDON : HODDER AND
STOUGHTON   *x*   *x*   27
PATERNOSTER ROW : MCM

TO THE MOST NOBLE

MARQUIS OF NORTHAMPTON

MY FRIEND

IN ADMIRATION OF HIS COMMONSENSE CHRISTIANITY

THIS LITTLE BOOK

IS GRATEFULLY DEDICATED

BY FRANK T. BULLEN

PREFACE

IT may be objected by many who read these lines, that there is a great deal too much of the Ego in them. If so, I can assure the objectors that I sympathise with them deeply. That is my feeling exactly. Yet, when you come to think of it, apart from the fact that I was requested to put my experiences of religious life at sea in this personal form, there really seems to have been no help for it, unless I had set up a fictitious personage and given him my real experiences. This would have been pleasanter for me, no doubt; would have saved me from many sarcastic remarks, &c.; but it would, I fear, have defeated the object for which I was asked to write.

I confess I am hopeful about the future of this little book, more so than the circumstances would warrant perhaps, certainly much more so than I have ever been before with my other works. And for this reason. Works of religious fiction abound;

they are popular, in many instances deservedly so ; but—they are felt to be fiction, and are not accepted as real pictures of everyday life. In this regard, I have tried, with what ability and experience I have been able to gather, to give a plain real picture of religious life at sea. I feel deeply that my picture is imperfect, very imperfect ; for who can turn his own heart inside out for his fellow-men's inspection without being suspected of posing, insincerity, or some such striving after effect, much less rightly appraise the motives and actions of his shipmates ?

But one can at least try to be simple, truthful, and direct ; one can refuse to be ashamed to own himself a friend of Jesus Christ, or to avow himself a firm believer in the efficacy of prayer for amelioration of all the ills of life.

Lastly, it will be noticed that names and dates are given most sparingly, grudgingly. The reason for this is, I think, obvious. I do not fear libel actions, but I do dread giving unnecessary pain.

F. T. B.

Malta : *September* 1900.

CONTENTS

CHAPTER I

INTRODUCTORY

WITH the most hearty desire to plunge forthwith into the heart of my subject I am compelled to admit the necessity of a few preliminary remarks. For otherwise the question would at once arise, 'Under what influences did this man fall at that most plastic time of life when the young mind first awakens?' All readers who take an interest in that most important of all subjects, the rise and progress of godliness in the human soul, are properly most curious to know when, where, and how it was that any particular soul under discussion first began to feel the craving after God. To say that no two of such cases are exactly similar would be to utter an obvious platitude, and yet there are vast numbers of otherwise intelligent people who believe in machine-made Christians. Therefore it seems well

B

to remind them that there can be no such thing as a mechanical Christian, using the name in its reasonable sense. Mechanical religionists there are in abundance, but the very essence of Christianity is its spirituality as distinguished from mere mechanism.

In my own case, my earliest recollections of religion are indissolubly bound up with three things: First of all being taught by my aunt, who brought me up from infancy to the age of eight and a half years, to kneel at my bedside and say my prayers; next, at the age of four, my surreptitious reading of 'Paradise Lost'; and, lastly, regular attendance at the Lock Chapel in the Harrow Road, where, at a ludicrously early age, I became one of the choir on its first institution.

Now of these three early memories the first requires no comment, yet I dare to say that it was the most important of all. An early acquiring of the habit of prayer, even though it be only formal, must be one of the greatest benefits that a human being can receive. And where, as in my own case, it is accompanied by an earnest endeavour on the part of the teacher to make the young mind grasp the mighty fact of the existence of a Friend able to do anything for the asker, and never more pleased than when being asked confidently for favours quite outside of any human power to grant, its value as a factor in true life is quite beyond estimate. But my dear aunt was, although intensely Evangelical, a rigid formalist. To her mind the fear of God was of more importance than the love of God. He, the Almighty One, was not to be approached familiarly. Set forms and attitudes were as necessary as unwavering faith in order that prayers should be heard, and, although this was more implied than expressed, answer to prayer was quite a minor consideration. The great thing was the saying of prayers, the repetition of certain words got by heart, in a reverent and orderly way. He must not be troubled with requests for such temporal matters as payment of the rent when work was slack, or helping over a difficult task, whether lesson or work. 'Grace' was what He must always be petitioned for (and I did not know what grace was for many years after), and we must always remember that if it were not for Gentle Jesus coming between us and God we should not only never be heard, but, for our sins, we should be punished with such terrible things that they could be only summed up in one comprehensive word—hell.

How is it that I remember all these points so clearly? I do not know. I am aware that the child's memory is normally of wonderful tenacity, but there may have been another sufficient reason. My aunt was an old maid. And she had an intense horror of the foulness of the streets. So, although we were very poor, I was never allowed 'out to play.' Fortunately we had a large garden attached to the little house in Desboro' Terrace (now Marlborough Street), Harrow Road, where all my early years were spent, so that my health never suffered from close confinement, but I grew up with a habit of providing my own company, holding long conversations with myself aloud. And since the principal things of interest in my life were more or less connected with religion, that subject was almost always the theme of my solitary discussions. So I suppose it became inevitable that all I heard upon the subject should be stamped ineffaceably upon my memory. So much so that even to-day at any moment I can reproduce for myself a mental picture of my aunt, with spectacles on, solemnly reading her big Bible in our prim

little parlour with its horsehair-covered chairs, the
old mahogany loo-table with a curiously irregular
split running right across it, into which I used to
drop pins and wonder where they had gone, and
the faded Brussels carpet, threadbare in places,
pervading the whole floor. I say pervading, for
once I remember it being taken up. I came
suddenly into the room ignorant of what had
happened, and was horrified ; the place was foreign,
its very atmosphere was changed.

I used to sit facing her, my short legs dangling,
for those chairs had no rails in front, and holding
myself from slipping off the glassy seat by hook-
ing my elbows on the table. This made it
natural for me to press my palms against my
ears, and thus I discovered that I could at will
produce a variety of tone in the somewhat
monotonous reading without committing the
offence of fidgeting. An almost imperceptible
movement of my hands allowed the sound to pour
in, or to be shut out of, my ears, and this simple
feat gave me very much satisfaction.

I did not like the Bible. I cannot remember
at that time ever reading it for choice. That is
easy to understand. Bible reading was a task

that must be performed. Not to read so many verses every day, with treble or four times the quantity on Sunday, was to offend God greatly. Understanding what one read was desirable, of course, but not necessary—the great thing was to read. Therefore I took no interest in the Bible for a long time. I read it aloud. I stumbled over the Prayer Book version of the Psalms (which we always read in those days at the Lock Chapel turn-about with the minister), and was glad when the reading was done. Then there came a summer when, finding the mornings interminably long in bed, I took to climbing out and hunting for something to read.

I was always put to bed at seven, but as my aunt did not go to bed till midnight, getting up again was quite another thing. She, poor woman, was so tired with her dressmaking that her usual hour for rising was half-past eight or nine, and as until she got up I was also compelled to remain in bed, the time from four o'clock A.M. or thereabouts hung very heavy. On the mantelpiece there were a few books, of which I only remember a New Testament, somebody's advice to young servants, a cookery book, and a small copy of

'Paradise Lost.' The two latter I used to take into bed with me as silently as possible, for fear of disturbing my aunt, with whom I slept, and read. But the cookery book soon lost its interest, while the poem, in spite of its long, hard words, of its blank verse, and of its deep learning, fascinated, enthralled me. Let no one ever tell me again of such and such a book being beyond or above a child. Only let it be a good book, and you may safely leave it to the child's discretion, fancy, imagination, what you will. My recollections of the glamour that wonderful poem cast over me are almost poignantly pleasurable. It was all so real to me. I never for one instant doubted the absolute truthfulness of any part of the story, and I well remember how, after reading that part where Milton speaks of the Almighty hanging out in heaven His golden scales to decide whether the celestial armies should part or fight, that I went about softly, imagining the awful conflict impending in the air, and the mighty hand of God balancing the issues. I do verily believe that early devouring of Milton has tinged my whole life.

Presently came Sunday school, under the superintendence of the gentle lady to whom with

affectionate remembrance I have dedicated the
' Cruise of the " Cachalot." ' I do not remember
much of her teaching, because I was personally in
a class taught by a dentist named Barker, who,
with his brother, was a devoted friend of the
school. But Miss Hensley, as superintendent, was
beloved by all. Not one of us but felt prouder of
the privilege of being invited home to tea with her
on Sunday afternoon, and being honoured with
the burden of her cloak and bag of books, than as
if we had suddenly been called upon to command
a ship or drive a fire-engine. At that school, on
the bridge beneath which is Westbourne Park
Railway Station, I passed many a happy hour, but
I cannot recall any impression more definite than
that of the loveableness and the patience of the
teachers, and the general mischievousness of the
boys and girls.

May I say, without being suspected of egotism,
that I was a good little boy? I think so, because everyone will realise that under the firm,
wise, and kind rule of Auntie, it was most unlikely that I should be anything else. Most
likely I was a terrible little prig, and I have no
doubt but that I was cordially hated by the more

human boys, who were disgusted at my smug virtue, virtue that had never been put to the test but once, when it broke all to pieces. It was an awful downfall. I have said that we were very poor ; so that my perquisites being all the farthings that came into the house must have testified to great generosity on Auntie's part. But I was nót allowed to spend one on any pretence. They were all solemnly put into a tin box with a slit in the lid, whose sides were ornamented with bees busy hiving honey.

Now, whether, after I went to day-school at seven years of age, the sight of other boys spending money brought upon me a raging desire to do the same or not, I do not know. All I remember is that one night, having duly elaborated my plan of campaign, I carried up to bed with me an old knife and a pencil-box. And after having said my prayers and kissed Auntie good-night, I lay counting her retreating footsteps down the stairs. Then creeping out of bed I drew aside the blind so that the bright moonlight should stream in. And with hardened heart I tousled that money-box until quite a heap of farthings lay upon the bed-quilt. I did not take them all—just a few I left as a salve to my conscience or in the hope that the breaking-in would not be noticed. Then, placing the looted farthings in the pencil-case (one of the old-fashioned ones like a truncheon) I hid it away, crept into bed again, and went to sleep.

I awoke in the morning without a shade of remorse, only anxious to get out of the house with my plunder. That was easily managed, and at dinner-time, instead of coming home straightway, I called certain of my intimates to me, and together we invaded a shop where they sold ginger-beer, doubtful fruit, and sweet-stuff. I spent royally, enjoying to the full the delightful sensation for the first time. But I had so many farthings (nearly two shillings'-worth) that there were still many left at school-time. I told a lie about being kept in to account for my delay in appearing to dinner, and still I did not feel any compunction. During the afternoon at school I became so inordinately puffed up at the exalted pinnacle I had reached in the estimation of my school-fellows (as I fondly imagined) that I waxed reckless and arrogant. I brandished my pencil-case, rattling the wealth it still contained, when suddenly the lid flew off, and in a jingling shower of bronze the farthings flew in every direction all over the schoolroom floor.

The memory of the inquiry that followed is still painful. How step by step my iniquities were unveiled, how eagerly the partakers of my bounty gave evidence against me, until, under guard, I was marched home and handed over to my aunt, with a full account of what had happened. Then came the hardest part to bear. Auntie cried ; and she was not given to tears as a rule. She cried bitterly to find that after all her care, her charge had suddenly developed into a thief and a liar. Then feeling that it was her duty so to do, she bought a penny cane and beat me, every blow, I am sure, hurting her far more than it did me. The whole episode was a landmark, and the lessons it taught exceedingly valuable. The most valuable of all, of course, did not appeal to me then as it does now, viz. that cloistered virtue is impotent, that inability to steal does not make a thief honest, and that ignorance is by no means innocence.

But I must get on. There came presently that dread event about which I cannot think even now without a shudder—my sudden hurling out of this haven into a troubled sea of violence. Imagine, if you can, what it must have meant to a child such as I was, at the age of nine, being transferred without a word of warning from the atmosphere of my aunt's quiet, godly home to a London laundry of over thirty years ago in Kensal New Town. The language I now heard continually was truly almost unintelligible at first, but I soon began to learn what it meant. There were a dozen women employed—coarse, shameless, and in their talk as lewd as any sailors I have ever been shipmate with. Moreover, I was tried physically. From being so tenderly cared for that I was hardly expected to wash myself, I was now made to turn the mangle and wringing-machine, to scrub the dirtiest of the dusters, &c., to go long, weary journeys with parcels such as I could carry, and do all to a running accompaniment of blows and abuse and shortness of food. My hours were from six in the morning until eleven at night, except on Sundays, when I sat, like Cinderella, after the dinner things had been washed up and put away, by the ashes of the kitchen fire, with no other company than the black-beetles and crickets. No more church or Sunday-school now. But I still kept up the habit of saying my prayers, though it never occurred to me to ask God for deliverance. That was entirely due, I know, to the way in which, as I have before hinted at, it had been instilled into my mind that we were only to ask for spiritual blessings from our Father, except in the disciple's prayer, which, of course, became perfunctory from innumerable repetitions. I may have been told that it was a good thing to ask God for anything I wanted and confidently look for a prompt answer to my request, but if so I have no recollection thereof whatever.

But although I made no audible moan, my dumb longings were great. Some day, but not just yet, I may attempt a description of those dreadful days, extending over nearly three years, during which I struggled against the fate that I felt was undeserved, yet did not know how to escape. Then I became familiar with all forms of evil, all expressions that men and women use in a sort of ignorant defiance of the Unseen Powers they fear and hate. A sort of act of spiritual suicide, I suppose. But I did not talk like that myself, and I still said my prayers, although nobody knew down here, nor did I myself know why I kept up the practice.

Then came the second great change in my life—I went to sea. The plain bald facts of my going I have related in the 'Log of a Sea Waif,' but I have not told, because I am not able to tell, of my utter loneliness and heart-hunger. I could not help but feel that liberty lay before me, freedom from starvation and all the vicissitudes of an Arab life ashore, but the sea loomed before me as a vast desert, all unknown. I had no friends on board the ship, and when, as we left the dock-head, the mate's wife—a comely Shields woman—stooped and kissed me, saying, 'God bless ye, ma puir chiel,' my heart overflowed in a few unaccustomed tears. Boys, such as I then was, do not weep much as a rule : they learn to endure hardness early, and without pitying themselves too greatly.

As I watched the familiar landmarks of London recede, I felt more wretched than I have ever done before or since. True, I was leaving no friends, I had no single tie, but neither had I any enthusiasm for the sea—only dread, only a sick feeling of doubt and terror. London represented to me all that I had ever known, its very stones were familiar acquaintances, and in default of human friends I had grown, I suppose, much attached to inanimate things.

On board the ship little notice was taken of me for the first day. I was cabin-boy, my duty being to attend upon the captain, mate, and second mate, under the orders of the mahogany-faced old man who was supposed to fill the double office of cook and steward. All that I had to do I could do fairly well, for housemaid's work was perfectly familiar to me, and it did not over-tax my puny strength. But I was not of use long. Even before we left the river, the smell of the foul little cuddy almost made me ill, and from it I was unable to escape, as most of my work lay there. When, however, we cleared the Nore and were being dragged ruthlessly seaward by a powerful tug-boat in the teeth of a rising gale, when white sheets of spray swept from one end of the miserable old barque to the other, so that there was no dry corner to be found except in the cuddy, I felt as if I was going to die. I remember creeping like a hurt dog under the quarter of the long-boat which was lashed on the main hatch, and there, wet to the skin and kept so by the never-ceasing spray, I passed into a comatose state at the bottom of a pit of misery, to which death himself would have come as an angel of deliverance.

Such an experience would, I venture to assert, be impossible to-day. For a mere child of between eleven and twelve to be thus left to live or die as it might chance, without anyone caring, without anyone coming to see, would not be permitted on board any ship now. Yet I was esteemed fortunate in being left alone. I know of cases where boys as ill as I then was have been hunted out of a lair like mine with blows and curses and driven aloft. To the throes of their sickness was added the agony of fear, clinging to the swaying rigging in the blackness of the night amid the howling of the angry wind. This was spared me. Afterwards, when I had grown stronger, I was often sent aloft to tasks too heavy for me, and far away up in the air have felt all my energies depart in the weakness of seasickness, not daring to come down and leave the sail unfurled. But now I was at least suffered to lie quietly and endure.

In saying that I was utterly neglected, I did one poor creature an injustice—a negro lad, five or six years older than myself, who was also in evil case, nipped by the bitter wind of an English February, and beaten frequently by anyone who chose to exercise the shameful privilege. When I recovered consciousness—I don't know how long after my first creeping in there—I found Jem sitting by my side, endeavouring to coax me into swallowing a morsel of soaked biscuit and drink a drop of water. Sententiously and with a quaintness that I found irresistibly funny after I got well, he was quoting the Bible to me. I found when I got to know him that he had been a Sunday-school teacher at home in Jamaica, which accounted for his knowledge of Holy Writ, but did not account for the delightful way in which he applied it to every circumstance of his daily life.

'Naow, leetle boay, you mus' eat somefin, 'r else yew gwine die. An' den, yew know, yew gwine be all right, ob co'se ; but yo duty tords Gord am ter lib s' long s' ever yew kin. Wy, yewse mos' s' highly favered 's me. 'Oom de Lord lobef He chasenef, 'n skurjef ebery son 'oom He recebef, don' y' know ? Now dey isn't many folks roun' dat's a-getting maw skurjin dan I is jes now, 'n sence de dear Lord less de mate go on wid it, well den de Lord Hesef 'sponsible, see ! So I feels

C

laik a son fo' shuah, a son wuts belobed, too—now mine I tole yer. 'N yew, wy, bress Gord, youse bein' chaysen too. Nudder way, ob co'se. De good Lord knows better dan treat all his chillen de same ; but neb' mine, you'se a son, an' a deah son too. Don' you leggo dat ar.'

So he talked away, the mere fact of his presence comforting me, apart from his cheery talk, until at last I managed to swallow a few morsels. And then that poor fellow prayed such a prayer as I had never heard before. Strange chills ran through me as I listened, a kind of awe at the fact that here was a man, and a black man at that, who seemed to be on more intimate terms with Almighty God than was safe. He talked to God, reminded Him of all sorts of things, at the same time admitting that it was not possible for Him to forget anything concerning the least of His creatures, but emphasising the fact that it did himself good to tell so sympathetic a listener all that was in his mind. He prayed for everybody on board, especially for the captain, who, he said, needed most to be prayed for, because he was probably the worst of all the crew ; but for me he reserved his final effort. And when he had finished, I was better ; I had been educated into the high knowledge that henceforth prayer was not merely the repetition of certain formulæ, but a real means of communication between God and my small self. That I didn't even need to kneel down and fold my hands and shut my eyes, or even speak aloud.

This, coming upon all that had gone before, was of the most inestimable benefit to me. I was not miserable any longer. My mind was fortified, and my body soon accommodated itself to the motion of the apple-sided old vessel, so that I was able to get about my work. I liked the cabin no better, for I could not get used to the foulness of its atmosphere nor its mental gloom. There was no conversation held between the officers and the skipper. They sat at their meals in grim silence as if bound by some awful rule to waste no word upon each other. The only place where I might legitimately go for companionship was the galley ; but the cook, though talkative enough, and, in a ferocious way, inclined to be companionable with me, could only express himself in terms that were almost entirely filthy or blasphemous, while his tales were of a kind that were painful to hear, apart from the language in which they were told.

Now I had been expressly forbidden to go into the men's quarters—the fo'csle. It was so bad a place to be in, leaky, dark, and mephitic, that one would hardly have thought any prohibition necessary, but there was cheerfulness and animated conversation there. Besides, the men spoke as kindly to me as they were able. In fact, all the kind words I got came from them ; and lastly, Jem, the negro boy, was there. So gradually I took to creeping forward after dark, and sitting in the fo'csle with the men, interested beyond measure by their conversation (which was not always of the cleanest), and feeling at times quite satisfied with my lot. This, of course, could only have one ending. I was soundly flogged, and threatened that if ever I went into the fo'csle again I should be cast out of the cabin altogether. For a week I abstained, until the misery of the cabin grew unbearable, and again I transgressed. Another rope's-ending, and then banishment, to my exceeding delight ; my satisfaction fully compensating me for my bruises.

Thus I became a fo'csle hand, and never but once, and that only for a short passage, have I filled a steward's place since.

CHAPTER II

RELIGIOUS LIFE IN THE FO'CSLE

In becoming a denizen of the fo'csle, I entered unconsciously upon the fourth great change in my life. Of the first I cannot now speak; it happened before my memory was born; the second was that sorrowful out-casting from the serene haven of my aunt's home into the tempest-tossed sea of the laundry and the streets; the third was going to sea. But this last change was, I think, the most momentous of all. For I was now, at an age when most boys are mere children, admitted to the real companionship of men on such terms of equality as few boys ever experience until they can be rightly called boys no longer.

The circumstances were peculiar. All the conditions of service in this old ship were so bad, food and accommodation being alike abominable and her hull and rigging so rotten, that it was constructive murder to send her to sea. Had the

master and officers been genial, sympathetic men,
determined to make the best of things and doing
their best to hearten up the ill-used crew, much
might have been done to lighten the gloom. But
the skipper's temper was morose and vindictive.
His face wore a continual scowl, and he never
spoke to anyone, even the mate, without arousing
a bitter feeling of resentment in their breasts by
his opprobrious words.

So that his treatment of me was taken by the
fo'csle hands as a studied insult to them, as one
more item in the black account against him, and
they determined to do what in them lay by their
treatment of me to annoy him. All agreed to pet
me and make my life in the fo'csle as happy as it
could well be. And in my watch on deck, whenever I was given a task they considered too hard
for me, one of them would rather ostentatiously
come to my assistance, all the more readily if the
old man were in sight. In my watch below I was
always being taught something useful. The mysteries of knots, splices, seizings, bends, cringles,
and all the manifold intricacies of sailorising were
unfolded to me with the greatest patience and
kindness, although the teachers often squabbled

among themselves over the exact method in which this or that piece of work should be done. One man, a big Yorkshireman we called Joe, laid himself out to teach me the mending and making of clothes, neglecting his own sewing, and making what he called a 'tarpaulin muster,' that is, a general collection from his watchmates of any old garments they could spare to fit me up with what I sorely needed, sufficient clothes.

Looking back upon that time years after I have often thought with deepest feeling of the behaviour of those rough, almost savage men. They modified their language for my sake. If I entered the fo'csle during the telling of one of the usual tales of a 'Highway' debauch there was an instant hush, nor, although one or two of them grumbled a little at first about it, was this practice ever altered while that crew were together. I had nothing to give them in return but affection, and with that I was overflowing; because for years it had been dammed up without ever getting an opportunity to flow at all. Now that I was amongst the kindest of friends I did not know how to make enough of them or to show my love, until one day I was crooning to myself one of the hymns I had learned at the Lock Chapel : 'When gathering clouds around I view,' to the tune of 'Melita.' When I had finished I noted how intent the silence was, and looked around abashed. But one of the chaps said : 'Got 'ny more like that, Tommy?' and delighted, I tuned up in earnest. After that in the dog-watches my treble pipe was always in request, although with the exception of 'Mother kissed me in my dream,' 'What are the wild waves saying?' and 'Little Nell,' I knew nothing but hymn tunes. The men's great favourite was Jackson's 'Te Deum,' which I used to sing at the very pitch of my lungs.

Now whether this singing of the songs of Zion had any effect upon the men beyond mere outward alteration of conversation and conduct never troubled my mind, because I knew nothing at all about the matter. With me it was merely a revival of pleasant memories, of emotional delights, just as saying my prayers was a performance due solely to habit. But Jem's lessons in the all-round efficacy of prayer had not been without their effect, so that now I used to ask in such language as I could command for what I considered would be good for my friendly shipmates. My greatest friend was

Yorkshire Joe, who taught me tailoring, and his welfare formed the central subject of my petitions. But to my great grief he was subject to furious gusts of passion, when he would swear horribly, using language that I had never heard until I came to sea, language wherein the names of Jesus, of God, and of Hell were combined in such fantastic blasphemy that I trembled to my heart, expecting momentarily to see him fall dead. So it came about that one night when I was repeating my usual requests to the Invisible Father in whom I most fervently believed, I received a startling testimony. I suppose I must have been a little more emphatic and unconventional than usual, for when I had finished I saw Joe standing by my side, his rugged, bronzed face all a-work, and his beard sparkling in the feeble rays of the lamp as if it had been sprinkled with dew.

Full of concern I asked him what was the matter. But he returned an evasive reply, putting his hand upon my head and remaining quite silent afterward for several moments. Then suddenly he asked: 'Why was ye a-praying for me, Tommy?' Something tugged at my heart, and bursting into tears, I faltered out: 'Because—

because I'm so fond of you, Joe—you've been so kind to me, and I was afraid God would strike you dead some day if you didn't leave off asking Him to. I do wish you wouldn't swear so dreadfully : it does frighten me so !' He listened in perfect silence and then said gravely and slowly : 'Well, I won't any more—you see if I do. Not that I mean anythin' by it, it's only a way of speakin' I've got into, an' I hardly know when I do it. But what was you really afraid of, little man ?' 'I was afraid that God would kill you and put you in Hell for ever and ever,' I panted. 'Ah !' he murmured, 'but suppose——' and then he stopped suddenly. After a little while he said, quite gently and low, 'Let me hear ye say them prayers agen, will ye ?' Very shyly, and in an almost inaudible whisper, I repeated my prayers while he leaned over my hammock—the hammock he had made and swung for me because I had no bed and he would not let me lie on the hard bunk-boards—and when I had finished he said quite clearly and solemnly, 'Amen.'

I wish I could say that from that day forward he was cured of his blasphemy, but it would not be true. There is only one cure for a habit like that, and it had not been applied.   Nevertheless, he strove hard against the violence of his tongue, and I have often seen him when just about to give way glance around at me standing near and be silent his sunburnt face flushing a deeper red.

Now the conversation in the fo'csle took a decidedly theological turn. We had not a Bible on board, as far as I knew, certainly not one in the fo'csle, so that it was impossible to bring any evidence to bear upon the discussions that took place, and in consequenee some extraordinary views were aired. Strange to say, there were no quarrels over the arguments. I say 'strange' because every sailor knows that argument about religion in a ship's fo'csle is perhaps the most fruitful cause of rows there. So much so that in many fo'csles the subject is tabooed altogether. I have heard men whose lives were as foul as a man's life could well be contending furiously over particular forms of religion, the true church to go to, the real priesthood, &c., while it was evident that they did not possess the slightest knowledge of the subject they were discussing with so much heat. Still less had they any real care for the truth. Poor fellows !

But in the ' Arabella's ' fo'csle religion was discussed quietly, and although I heard many remarks that made me shiver, they sounded so dreadful to my carefully tutored ears, the familiarity with which those lofty themes and holy names was handled had in it nothing of irreverence. On one point they were all agreed. It was that there was no hell for sailors. They were not at all sure that a good many shipowners would escape the unquenchable fire, especially those who gave liberally to charities ashore and fed their wage-earners at sea worse than pigs. In fact, some of them went so far as to say that if there wasn't a hell for such people there ought to be. None of them had any doubt as to the existence of God. That matter was discussed at great length, the idea of such a doubt existing being apparently only stated to be demolished with scorn. About the Fall they held some curious notions, which I do not feel justified in stating here—because I am not able to write them in Greek. Indeed, I did not at the time quite realise their meaning. Some years afterwards, however, I came across an old book in New Zealand which gave an account of this particular heresy as having been in full vigour about 200 years after Christ.   Since then I have heard nearly every one of those strange old perversions of great truths put forward by unlettered men and women, both at sea and ashore, proving, to me at least, that the minds of men in all ages run in very much the same grooves when they give the rein to their fancy in matters of religion.

As to the Plan of Salvation they knew next to nothing.   Dim and hazy ideas of the vicarious sacrifice of Christ for man were somewhat timidly hazarded, but of the great fundamental truth of Christianity, summed up in the words, ' God was in Christ reconciling the world unto Himself,' they had not the shadow of an idea.   I said but little at these discussions, unless asked a question ; and, truth to tell, I took no great amount of interest in them, beyond feeling the importance of being permitted to nestle in the midst of the talkers by the side of my friend Joe.   But I have no doubt that the free handling of topics which in my own experience had been confined to Sunday for as long as I had heard them mentioned at all had, on the whole, a beneficent influence upon me, although its effects were not manifested for some years.

Stormy days were ahead.   First of all came a

row between Joe and the skipper, a row which had myself for its proximate cause. Joe took upon himself to go aft and ask the 'old man' for a piece of second-hand canvas wherewith to make me a 'jumper,' a primitive kind of garment like a cuirass, which, when lined with a piece of old flannel, makes a very warm shelter and requires little clothing underneath. This piece of impudence, as the skipper termed it, led to hot words between Joe and himself, much to the delight of the rest of the crew. For me personally it had unpleasant results. For the skipper, at the first opportunity, beat me unmercifully, which most unfair exercise of authority nearly ended in a mutiny. I declare that I was in no sense to blame. Had I been consulted I would certainly have endured any extremity of cold before giving my consent to the skipper's being asked for canvas. And when I paid the penalty I did so feeling greatly afraid lest the crew should do anything dreadful in their indignation at the way in which their pet was being treated. When I got forward, although writhing with pain, I implored Joe not to do anything—I looked upon him as capable of any act of violence for all his tenderness to me—

and, very reluctantly, he yielded to my impor-
tunities.

Shortly afterwards we arrived in Georgetown,
Demerara, and I had a most pleasant time in
harbour, the skipper being generally ashore, and
the mate, a Norwegian, being far too much in
awe of the crew, who were all English but Jem
the Jamaican negro, to interfere much with
me. Then came 'liberty day,' when the crew,
watch by watch, received a little money on account
of their wages, and were permitted to spend twenty-
four hours ashore. Having heard a great deal in
the fo'csle of the intentions of the men I was much
afraid of what would happen when they returned.
They now discussed with loosened tongues their
prospective pleasures, while I listened with awe,
wondering why they did not restrain one another
before me as I had seen them do previously.

At last, I went to Joe just as he was ready to
depart, and implored him, for my sake, not to get
drunk and come on board to fight. He promised
me with a smile that he would not, and he kept
his word. He was the only sober man out of the
fo'csle members of the crew on the morning of
their reassembling, and when the mutiny took

place, whose events I have fully recorded in the
'Log of a Sea Waif,' he alone held aloof. And I
was able to save his life. For if it had not been
for my shouted warning he would certainly have
been stabbed by an Irishman, who, one of the
pleasantest of men at other times, was then simply
frantic with new rum.

The result of that grim morning's work was
that all of the old crew, except Joe and Black Jem,
went to prison; even the old cook and steward
departed to the place which I had long thought
secretly was the only home he was fit for. Of
course, a new crew had to be shipped at once, for
we were bound away. They came, a very different
lot from those we had on the passage out. The only
really nice man among them was the cook, a little
fair Irishman, with a long auburn beard, who was
mightily disgusted at finding that the skipper had
shipped a Chinaman as steward, who would, by
ship etiquette, be his superior. But none of them
was so utterly abandoned and grossly animal as a
cadaverous young fellow, who said that he was a
Eurasian. His manners, his language, his looks
were alike beastly. Him Joe tackled two days
after leaving port, and, much to my terror and
discomfort, gave him a terrible thrashing.

All the old pleasantness of the fo'csle was now gone, and in its place ribaldry and lewdness reigned supreme. Joe and I spent much time together away from the rest, and if I could only recall some of our conversations, they would surprise myself in their innocent outpouring of all that was good in either of our hearts. I clung to the big man as my sole defender from what I felt would be much discomfort, if not cruelty, and he repaid my confidence beautifully, not allowing even a threat to be made against me without instant interference, and as his size and strength gained for him great respect I was left unmolested. In return for his protection I believe that my companionship was a real solace to him. He became daily more grave and thoughtful, and tried to recall from his long experience such anecdotes as he thought would please me or be good for me to hear. I asked him multitudes of questions about the beautiful strange things that were daily appearing in sea and sky and on the shores we skirted on our way down to the ports in the Gulf of Mexico, where we were to load mahogany for home. But to the majority of my questions he was fain to admit that he knew

D

no answers. He owned that he had so long been blind and deaf to the sights and sounds of the sea that, although he was now beginning to take an interest in them which surprised him, he was almost as ignorant of their meaning, their causes, and their lessons as I was. And he was not a reading man. Though fairly intelligent, and a splendid workman, he spent his leisure entirely in the care of his scanty wardrobe and in making little models of ships, at which latter pleasant pastime he was an adept. With a vast amount of patient labour he had constructed a model of the Downs, that magnificent roadstead off Deal that used to be an anchorage for hundreds of outward or homeward bound ships before steam became the chief motive power in ocean traffic. He had made out of putty a relief model of the shore at one side of a large board, upon which he had, in its proper place, represented the sea by a painted groundwork. Dotted here and there over the green surface were half models of variously rigged vessels under sail, securely pinned down to the board on their flat sides, and with all their sails carved out of wood.

At this task had he worked strenuously, but he

was destined never to finish it. For when we arrived in Sant' Ana we found the place to be a veritable Alsatia. No law, no order, every man doing that which was right in his own eyes, and wages for seamen abnormally inflated. And Joe was getting very tired of this miserable old vessel of ours. He had never made chums with any of the new crew ; between him and the skipper there was at the best but an armed neutrality, which at any time would certainly have broken out into fierce persecution of Joe by the old man had the former shown any sign of weakness. At last one night I felt in my sleep somebody kiss me. I remembered it distinctly afterwards, but at the time it was insufficient to arouse me thoroughly. In the morning there was a terrible outcry. The old man, taking his constitutional on the poop, as he always did before six o'clock, found the stout rope which had held our longboat astern hanging straight down, the longboat being gone. All hands were immediately called aft, when it was at once seen that Joe and Harry, a Newfoundlander, were absent. The wrathful skipper turned upon me savagely, demanding information concerning Joe. I had none to give, or, I fear, miserable little coward that I was, I should have supplied it. For now I knew there was no one to stand between me and any brutality that might be practised upon me. Trembling, I protested the exact truth, that I knew nothing of Joe's intentions or his movements, and with a fierce threat the skipper turned away. Then, mounting the rigging, he swept the horizon with his glass, discovering the boat drifting seaward seven or eight miles out. I should have said that we were anchored in an open roadstead, in company with some twenty other vessels, and that there was no shelter of any kind to seaward of us, nothing but the open waters of the Gulf.

The boat was recovered after a weary morning's row under that fervent sun, but her passengers were not found. Two days after, however, our skipper saw them both at work in the rigging of an American brig, anchored about half a mile distant from us. He went to claim them, but was not allowed on board, her skipper treating him to a great deal of sarcastic information. He returned on board foaming but helpless. Then poor black Jem, who was leading a terrible life in the fo'csle, came aft and demanded his discharge, which he was fully entitled to—indeed, he should have been set free in Demerara. He got it and his pay, some fifty dollars in silver. He packed up his few belongings and departed for the shore with ten dollars in his pocket ; the rest, at the suggestion of his shipmates, he left with one of them for safety. And when he came on board again and asked for his little hoard, they jeered at him and denied all knowledge of his money.

From all of which it may, I think, be fairly gathered that the ' Arabella's ' fo'csle was a bad place now to be in. As yet I was safe from physical ill-usage, because the little Irish cook, having grown very fond of me, had taken me under his protection. In fact, his affection for me was only equalled by his hatred of the Chinese steward, hatred which culminated one day in a murderous affray between them, after which the Chinaman was bundled ashore. I used to spend now all my spare time in the galley with the cook. He was a fervent Catholic, and used to tell me legends of the Saints, which to my mind were more interesting than the wildest romances I had yet read, besides being invested with a charm that was wholly the narrator's own. He also taught me many prayers to the Saints (as I thought), and fragments of Latin, making a queer jumble of impressions on my mind. But whatever our conversation turned upon, I bear witness that I never heard one word from that fiery tempered little ship's cook that might not have been spoken in the holiest company. He was one of nature's gentlemen, and would have scorned to sully a young mind by the transference to it of any dirt that might unhappily have accumulated in his own.

But another great change was at hand, although I had not the slightest inkling of its approach. I was getting fairly strong and wiry, tanned like an Indian from constant exposure to the fierce sun of Mexico; my feet, which had never known a covering since leaving England, were as hard as a negro's, and I knew my work very well. Besides these things I was rapidly learning to talk the prevailing language I heard around me—Spanish, which, though exceedingly useful, had one serious drawback—its utterly horrible misuse in swearing. And as the vilenesses of a foreign tongue which is picked up colloquially are always acquired first and retained longest, so I found my memory presently loaded with expressions that were always rising to my lips and frightening me almost beyond bearing by their horror. I came to the conclusion very soon that what I had taken for the worst language possible spoken in my own tongue was but as the prattle of infants compared with the hideous outrage on speech perpetrated by an angry Dago—I will not say Spaniard, since the mixed medley of Latin races there all spoke Spanish.

Then one morning I suddenly received a summons to come aft and speak to the skipper. I went in fear and trembling, for I was always in dread of a thrashing for something, I did not know what, but was quite sure that some reason could always be found for beating me. This time, however, my fears were quite groundless. The skipper received me as kindly as it was in his cross-grained nature to do, and informed me that he had made arrangements with a friend of his, who commanded a fine barque, the 'Discovery,' which was loaded and ready for sailing homeward, to take me with him. He gave me as his reason for thus sending me away that the 'Arabella' was never likely to reach home. She was so shaky, so utterly unseaworthy, that the probability was that she would become a wreck before getting clear of the Gulf, and he did not want to run the risk of having me drowned, as I was his brother's son. So I was to get ready at once and go on board my new ship with him that morning.

I was delighted at the prospect; boy-like, I did not speculate upon the probability of being worse off than I was now. In fact, had I thought about that side of the matter at all—I don't remember whether I did or not—I should no doubt have arrived at the conclusion that any change must be for the better. So I gathered my few belongings (be sure I was not overloaded with them), and departed with a shake of the hand and a ' God bless you ! ' from the cook, but not another sign of leave-taking from any other member of the crew. Arriving on board the ' Discovery ' I was amazed ; she was so grand a ship as compared with the wretched old hulk I had left. Her skipper received me very kindly and handed me over to the steward ; my uncle left me without a word of farewell, and I began life on board my second ship.

If I had been in danger of injury by too much hardship before, I was now likely to be spoiled by overmuch petting. Everyone on board was kindness itself. They seemed to look upon me as a plaything sent specially for their amusement. I had no regular duties. I lived in the cabin and revelled in the excellent food provided, luxuries which I had hitherto only dreamed of. I came and went through the fo'csle as I chose, no one interfering with me. My life was as completely changed as it was possible for it to be. But as far as religion went, the ' Discovery ' was frankly pagan. I never heard a word from any member of her crew that showed any recognition of God as a factor in the lives of men. The crew were a mixed crowd of foreigners and British, but pulled very well together, and, on the whole, she was what a sailor would call a comfortable ship. The one black spot in the pleasant scheme of things was the skipper's drunkenness. One of the most amiable of men, and withal, by the common consent of the crew, a first-class seaman, he drank so incessantly as to be never really sober. And this failing of his had its inevitable effect upon the crew in relaxing discipline, and making them all feel that they could do pretty much as they liked. I have often wondered since that they behaved as well as they did.

But it is time to bring this chapter to a close. I cannot help feeling that its title is somewhat misleading, since of religious life in the fo'csle or the cabin there was hardly a trace. Sunday was observed as a day on which no avoidable duties were performed on behalf of the ship. It was, however, looked upon as the time for washing and mending clothes, for doing, in fact, anything that a man wished to do for himself and did not care to take time for from his watch below. Any encroachment upon this privilege was fiercely resented, but only because it was felt to be a right that law provided for, and not in the least upon any moral or religious grounds. And, as I have already said, on board the 'Arabella' there was no Bible, and, with the exception of black Jem and the Irish cook, no man appeared to have God in his thoughts at any time, except as the subject matter for discussion in the dog-watch *causeries*.

CHAPTER III

GODLESS DAYS

I COME now to a long period, during which I am compelled to say that religious thoughts, as far as I could tell, and religious practices certainly, as far as my surroundings were concerned, were entirely non-existent. How far I am justified in briefly touching upon the leading incidents of those years I do not know. The general title of these reminiscences would seem to suggest the leaving out of those voyages wherein there was not to be found one spark of the recognition of the presence of Christ on board. Rather would it seem as if this particular part of my narrative should be headed: 'Without Christ at Sea.' Only I am sure that, firstly, such a title would be misleading, since the poor unthinking seafarer, although he omits to cultivate in the smallest, most perfunctory measure the acquaintanceship of Christ, forgets Him, in fact, as completely as he is able to do, can no more sail without Him than he can sail without water. And even though the name of Christ be unused, except to give weight to a meaningless oath or to emphasise a story, and His brotherly attributes are all unknown, there at any time may suddenly arise a deep, sincere longing after Him as the one faithful powerful Friend.

Secondly, it would be unjust to those who I trust will read these lines, to allow them to think that there is on board of every ship some form of religious observance, some recognition, however formal, of the overlordship of the Most High God. Unjust because misleading, hindering effort, and encouraging that lack of knowledge about the conditions of life in our merchant ships which is such a prominent and painful feature in our mental exercises to-day in Britain.

There is another difficulty in the way. As I have in the ' Log of a Sea Waif' dealt chiefly with these years about which I am now speaking, not, if I may coin a word, ' fictionising ' their incidents, but giving them as they occurred to the best of my recollection, it must occasionally happen that

I shall be travelling over old ground. I hope, however, that as I am on a different subject I may be forgiven for sometimes touching upon matters already dealt with elsewhere. So with this brief apologia I return to the 'Discovery.'

We left Sant' Ana the next day after I joined her, and for a fortnight I enjoyed life as I had never done before. Sailing upon summer seas with nothing but kindness shown me by all, and abundant leisure to indulge in what was always my delight, hanging over the side gazing into the limpid blue waters with their inexhaustible store of wonders, I was supremely happy. And then came an awful night, when I was suddenly awakened to the knowledge that the ship was wrecked—run ashore upon a coral reef in the middle of the Gulf while all hands, including the helmsman and the look-out man, were asleep. Even then, after the first shock had passed, I found that there was nothing to fear. The prospect of spending some time upon a little barren patch of sand had nothing in it alarming. Getting ashore was a trying experience, for the wind and sea had risen, and only by a series of hairbreadth escapes did we all succeed in getting safe to land.

Then came a few days of unalloyed pleasure. A free, wild life, such as boys pent up in cities pant after as they read stories of adventure, without any hardships at all. The days were spent in roaming round our small domain, picking up and throwing away such treasures in the way of shells, curious fish, and corals as are only seen in museums at home. So happy was that time that I felt quite loth to leave it when a friendly Frenchman, homeward bound from Vera Cruz to Bordeaux, hove to off the island, sent his boat ashore, and took most of us, including myself, away. Swiftly she bore us to Havana, where we were landed and placed in the British Consul's charge to await trans-shipment home at the earliest opportunity.

But the spirit of adventure was growing upon me, and without a thought of the consequences I left the company of my shipmates and became a hanger-on at the billiard-room of a large hotel much frequented by English and American skippers. Here, under these pleasant but baneful conditions, I rapidly developed into a pert boy, without reverence or fear, because I was encouraged to be saucy and witty by all who came.

And the only thing I learned which was of the slightest use to me was Spanish. But I was to have a serious call. The yellow fever devastated the city, and I could not help seeing how fast people's bodies were being carted away for burial. In the night, when except for the tolling of the great bell of the cathedral for the passing souls all was silent, I would often wake in a cold sweat of fear and pray that my life might be spared in the midst of all this death. This, however, was *only* fear. There was no sense of God's protecting care, no real desire for Him. After all, I was but a little boy of twelve living under abnormal conditions.

Not only was my life spared, but I had no illness of any kind during my stay of nearly six months. I witnessed company after company of miserable-looking recruits marched off into the interior to fight the Cubans; saw, too, their bleeding and tattered remnants come back. The sight of a dead man lying in the gutter of that great city became a familiar one; in fact, death in various forms was always prominent. And then came a hurricane, a terrible visitation in its destruction of shipping and dwellings, but a blessing in that it swept the city clean of the yellow scourge. A few days after the hurricane I was seized by the Vice-Consul and hurried on board a ship to be taken home. I pleaded to be allowed to remain, declaring that I had no home, but he would not listen, so again I took up the thread of board-ship life most unwillingly.

If religion had been conspicuous by its absence from the two previous ships, where my own countrymen were in the great majority, it could hardly be expected to show at all on board of my new vessel. For although she flew the British flag, being a Nova Scotian barque, she had the most extraordinary mixture of races in her small crew that I have ever known in one ship. I lived in the fo'csle, and I was there the sole representative of the British race. Three men of the near East, who called themselves Austrians, but of whom one was certainly a Montenegrin and the other two came from somewhere near Trieste; a Frenchman, a Swede, and four black men made up the fo'csle crowd, while the cook was an American negro and the carpenter a man whose nationality I never knew. Spanish was the language spoken in the fo'csle, but on deck orders were given in that extraordinary kind of English that is really the Lingua Franca of the sea. Of the 'afterguard,' the master was a gentle old Englishman, who had lived for some years in Cuba, holding some official appointment ; the mate was a drunken, loathly Scotsman, the only representative of that splendid race that ever I was shipmate with, of whom I could honestly say a hard word ; and the second mate a stern, seaman-like Englishman.

With such a crew as this it need hardly be wondered at that not even the husk of religion was present. It was never even mentioned in discussion. Instead, there were innumerable tales of devilry in the Levant, of bloodshed both afloat and ashore, until I used to wonder much what kind of a land it could be that bred such men as these. I never doubted the truth of their tales, for they all looked like men who would figure in such lurid exploits with the greatest delight, given the opportunity. Yet, strange to say, I was never on board of a more peaceful ship. Every man carried a murderous-looking knife stuck in a sash ; every man looked as if, on the slightest provocation, he would use it, and perhaps it was the mutual

E

respect bred by this knowledge of the price to be paid for quarrelling that kept things so uniformly peaceful. On deck it was the same. They were all good, willing seamen, quick and capable, and as no attempt was made to impose upon their good nature, things went very smoothly.

By this time I had almost lost the habit of prayer —my life in Havana on the whole was not favourable to its practice—thrown as I was into the midst of the wildest dissipation, kept up invariably until the small hours of the morning, and begun again about noon. But an event that occurred a week after we had sailed from Havana, bound to Mobile, made me revert to it in a great hurry. Whether through negligence on the part of the officers or the terrific swiftness with which it arose I do not know, but one morning we were suddenly stricken by a most terrible squall, a squall, in fact, of almost hurricane violence. I saw it coming, and it was as if the sea had reared itself into a wall of foam, which was rushing down upon us at incredible speed. All sheets and halyards were let go, but the sails would not come down, and the vessel went over, over, until her deck was almost vertical. I lay flat on the weather side with my feet against the side of the house feeling as if I were standing upright. And I heard beneath me the great stones composing the ballast rolling thunderously down to leeward as if to complete the vessel's destruction by turning her right over. I remember, as if it were even now happening, my feeling of utter helplessness of being saved, and I prayed for life, only a little more life. Overhead all was darkness and tumult, a tremendous confusion of noises which could not be separated by the ear, and beneath, that ominous rumbling. Suddenly the wind eased and the vessel righted a little. Speedily the sky cleared, revealing the state of affairs aloft. No spars had gone, but every rag of sail that had been set when the squall burst upon us—that is to say, nearly all the sail we carried—was gone, leaving only a few fluttering threads wrapped here and there about the lee-rigging. Well for us that the sails were an old suit and that the vessel was staunch. Had such an accident occurred to the ' Arabella ' she would have been blotted out like a burst bubble, and not one soul would have survived.

Now it settled down into a steady, fierce gale, making the work of bending fresh sails exceedingly toilsome and difficult.   All night long the men laboured cheerfully, doggedly, to get the vessel under control again by making it possible to set some sail, and when that was done they were sent below to shift the ballast, all of which they did without a murmur.   In all this labour I bore my small part, doing what I could until, tired beyond all expression, and aching in every limb from being so long drenched, the weather being very cold, I crept into a corner of the fo'csle that was allotted to me (I had no bunk) and fell fast asleep.

This was my first experience of bad weather at sea, so that no wonder need be manifested at its being so clearly stamped upon my memory, even though it is thirty years ago.   But one thing about the whole affair puzzles me, has often puzzled me since when repeated under similar circumstances— the calmness, almost amounting to indifference, with which, after the danger had passed, I looked upon the whole affair.   I should have expected to feel the deepest gratitude to God for answered prayer.   Instead of that I seemed to take it for granted that what had happened was only to be expected, and my thankfulness was far from being

commensurate with the fervour of my petition
when the danger was imminent. I have often
wondered whether this is a common experience, or
only a phase of individual ingratitude.

We arrived at our port without further adventure, except the losing of an anchor and sixty
fathoms of cable in a squall while anchored outside
the harbour waiting for a pilot, and as soon as we
had reached our loading berth the kindly old
skipper announced that the events of the last few
days had shown him that he was no longer fit to
command a ship, and that he intended to resign
and go home as a passenger in a steamer. I
believe everyone on board was genuinely sorry to
lose the old gentleman, who had endeared himself
to those rough fellows by his old-fashioned, kindly
ways. In his place we got a smart, bustling
Welshman, more than half a Yankee, who speedily
made himself felt on board, but who did not for
all that make the ship uncomfortable.

We filled up with cotton and started for home,
the time of year being January, and after six days
only found ourselves out in the Atlantic under
bare poles, writhing in the grip of one of the
tremendous winter gales. Poorly clad and badly

treated by the mate, I was very miserable. No work or hardship was spared me, and tasks beyond my strength were continually being given me. Nobody seemed to care what became of me except the little Frenchman, who in a variety of ways tried to lighten my burden in some measure, and lent me some of his own scanty stock of clothing. The gale lasted with scarcely any interval for a week, apparently increasing gradually in violence day by day until at last our vessel, large as she was, seemed to be but a toy-boat tossed from summit to hollow of these tremendous waves. I was full of terror, and consequently was instant in prayer for safety, but I got no real comfort until I considered how happy and unconcerned were the sea-birds hovering around. Then I thought that if they, so slight and frail, were safe from the raging of such a storm as this, surely we must be so likewise. And this reasoning, faulty as it was, gave me such confidence that I was never again frightened that passage : except when running before the next gale of wind at high speed we passed a sinking brig—saw her sink with all her crew, and were unable to help. Then indeed I felt afraid of the possibility of such a fate being ours. And after that awful sight I was unhappy, much more so than I should have been perhaps if I had found anyone to talk to about it. For although I could get along well enough with the queer Spanish spoken in the fo'csle (Spanish adulterated with Italian and French and scraps of other languages apparently as it suited the speaker) —get along, that is, in ordinary fo'csle talk—such conversation as I needed was not to be had.

We had another hair-raising incident when entering the Channel through following a strange vessel's lead in a dense fog. Only just by a few yards we succeeded in clawing off a deadly reef of rocks, the breakers boiling under her bows as she turned reluctantly away. After that there was no more trouble, and a few hours later the vessel was safely docked in Liverpool, and I was left alone on board, with the exception of an ancient watchman.

It is not that I desire to waste pity upon myself as I then was, but looking back I cannot help reflecting how sad a lot is that of the lonely, friendless child. Gregarious as we are by nature, there are few men and women who do not suffer a great deal when left without any human companionship, more especially if they have not realised the depth of the truth contained in the words, 'I will never leave thee nor forsake thee.' But for a child to learn by bitter experience that he or she is quite alone, with no one ever to cuddle up to, no one to come to for guidance and assistance at any time, is a hard matter. We often say that 'you can't put an old head upon young shoulders,' and, given normal conditions, the saying is true. There are exceptions, unfortunately. It *is* possible to put an old head upon young shoulders, but the process is a painful one, and its results are pitiful to see.

I might go on now to tell of the next two months spent ashore in Liverpool and London, trying in the intervals between the constant skirmishing around for something to eat and to 'get a ship,' and constantly being disappointed, but that the story does not belong to this connection. It must be sufficient to say that after many curious strugglings in those two great gatherings of human beings, I did at last succeed in obtaining a berth on board a barque bound to Jamaica as 'boy' at the good wage of 25s. per month. She was another pagan ship, and her crew the cruellest in all my experience. Usually, even in those days, there was sufficient public spirit, if I may call it so, in a ship's fo'csle to prevent a boy being ill-used *in* the fo'csle to any extent, although for impudence, laziness, or dirty habits, he would certainly be colted by some man with the approval of all the rest. But in this ship, from the big, loutish boy who was my colleague, to the oldest A.-B., all ill-treated me, until I became quite animalised, dully bearing what had become my lot without useless complaint. And I left off praying altogether. Why, I don't know, for certainly I needed it more than ever.

My misery came to an end by the vessel being wrecked on leaving the harbour homeward bound, and, taken all round, I had a fairly good time in Falmouth and Kingston before sailing for home (working my passage) in a large steamship. But as it was in Liverpool and in London, so it was here. I never came in contact with any religious influence at all. Being always in a more or less disrespectable condition as regards clothes, I did not dare to mingle with the well-clad worshippers going to church and chapel. For although I do not remember ever having been taught such a thing, in some mysterious way going to the house of God was in my mind indissolubly associated with fine clothes, and the idea of a shabby person being in church never occurred to me, or, if it did, only with a shudder of horror as at sacrilege. To this day the thought of going to church always brings back to me the faint, sweet scent of lavender and rose-leaves from the opening of drawers kept closed all the rest of the week. I hear the rustle of my aunt's ancient silk, to my reverent eyes a garment fit for a queen to wear. I see the great square enamel brooch with its gold border carefully being disinterred from its woolly bed to fasten her Paisley shawl with. The shilling for the collection (no other money might be carried on Sunday) lying ready on the toilet-cover to be slipped into her left-hand glove at the last moment. I smell again the eau de Cologne, as I am delighted by a few drops sprinkled upon my little handkerchief, which is then carefully adjusted with one corner sticking out of the breast-pocket of my Garibaldi. And then the sedate emergence from the house into the solemn outer air of Sunday, the sacred hush of the building, with its rows of Sunday-clad people, and the delicious thrill along the roots of my hair at the opening bars of the voluntary. Lastly, the entry of Mr. Forrest the vicar, and his curate, in their white robes, dimly associated, in my mind, with the garments of angels.

With such memories it is hardly to be wondered at that I shunned the church, and if, as possibly may have happened, I ever saw a humble conventicle with shabbily-dressed worshippers entering, I had been taught to regard such halls with horror as the meeting-places of a terrible class of people called ' Ranters,' who were only to be spoken of with a shudder.

On board the big steamer I came face to face with death in appalling guise, for yellow fever was raging in the last port we left—Port au Prince, in Hayti—and we had regularly two or three deaths a day for the first fortnight at sea. They were buried with the service of the Church, but I was always kept too busy to attend. I only got hurried glimpses of that most solemn of ·all religious services, a burial at sea.

I reached Liverpool penniless except for half-a-crown given me by a charitable Chinaman when I went ashore, and was again adrift in my own country. Once more I pass rapidly over my solitary wanderings in Liverpool until I again started seaward, this time in a big ship bound to the East Indies. Here, too, we were pagans. The only time on that long voyage that I ever heard the words of the Master was when we buried Peter Burn in the tropics, and the rendering of that last service to our shipmate made a very deep impression upon me, an impression I have striven several times to put into the printed word. Here, again, I was brought into close contact with death, for I was told off to nurse a man with small-pox, and I was with him alone when he died on the forecastle head of the ship as she came into Bimliapatam, on the Coromandel coast of India. But these impressions, solemn as they were, did not stay with me beneficially, as far as I am aware, and by the time we reached London I was becoming almost as much a pagan as any of my shipmates.

When I left the ship, however, I stayed in a boarding-house in the West India Dock Road, and presently found me a girl to walk out with. We only took two walks, however, for she disgusted me, and I no less disgusted her. In fact, she told me that I was such a molly-coddle that I ought to be taken out in a pram and fed from a 2–3 feeding-bottle. The fact was that my reverence for womenkind was so great, in spite of my experience, that I could not bear to hear any of them talk filth, and when my temporary sweetheart did so I reproved her with the gravity of an ancient monk, which, of course, was by no means to her taste.

I was now growing bigger and more confident. In consequence I found less difficulty in getting a ship, and soon I was outward bound to Australia in a huge American vessel, the crew of which, with the exception of three or four Scandinavians, were just a pack of gaol-birds. The skipper, too, was a very bad man—as bad a man, in fact, as ever I had the misfortune to come into intimate relations with. But I was speedily transferred from the fo'csle to the cabin, all unknown to the commander, and this move was a most valuable one. For the elderly Mulatto steward was an exemplary Christian, a man diligent in his business and of the meekest and most patient disposition. He took me entirely away from the abominations of the fo'csle, and in all ways that he could think of endeavoured to do me good. Some of his Biblical teachings and illustrations were almost as quaint in their misapplication as

those of my poor black friend Jem in the 'Arabella,'
but I never felt inclined to laugh—the old man
made me love him too much.

The desperadoes forward looted the cargo
continually, almost under the noses of the officers,
and the knowledge of their exploits made me
intensely glad that I was living clear of them, for it
looked to me as if they would be haled off to
prison as soon as we arrived.   And the companionship of the old steward compensated me for the
loss of all the life and movement that was going
on in the fo'csle.   He told me tales of the church
to which he belonged in America, of his great
favourite preacher Lorenzo Dow, of revivals, of
camp-meetings, while I sat enthralled at this
opening up to me of a totally unfamiliar phase of
life.

That was a time altogether good, and perhaps
all the sweeter from the knowledge that at any
moment the harsh voice and diabolical frown of
the skipper might break in upon our pleasant chat
and send us flying in different directions to obey
his commands.   I lived in mortal terror of him.
His scowl seemed to me so murderous, there
was such a wealth of hatred to all humanity,

as it appeared to me, in his black eyes with their penthouse brows, that the knowledge of his nearness to me was like a nightmare. So much did this terror grow upon me that, in spite of the affection I felt towards the steward, I made up my mind to run away as soon as I could after the ship's arrival in Melbourne. This resolution was confirmed by the wholesale desertion of the crew on the evening that we made fast at Sandridge Pier. When I saw how in spite of their deeds of robbery they got away unmolested, I set about packing up my belongings, and a day or two after, having arranged with the cook of one of the coasting steamers to stow me away for a passage to Sydney, I bade my old friend a most affectionate farewell and departed, making my escape without any difficulty.

Arriving in Sydney, I soon succeeded in getting a berth as lamp-trimmer in one of the coasting steamers, and for the next twelve months made a pretty complete circuit of the Australasian Colonies, living on the best of everything, earning good wages, learning all manner of things harmful to me, but never by any chance coming across anyone who was Christianly disposed, and feeling myself less and less anxious to seek after God. Often I would stand on deck when my ship was anchored in Sydney Harbour on Sunday morning and listen to the church bells playing ' Sicilian Mariners ' with a dull ache at my heart, a deep longing for something, I knew not what. But it never got the length of my going to church. I had good clothes now, but I had lost the desire. And I never prayed at all. My language was very bad, but somehow always stopped short of blasphemy because I was afraid of God. And some forms of grosser evil I shunned, also because I was afraid, not because my desires were not evil. Yes, it was a barren period.

CHAPTER IV

GODLESS DAYS (*continued*)

THIS easy life came to an end abruptly by my suddenly developing a longing to see England again. For the life of me I cannot tell why. There was apparently no reason why I should desire to return to the land of my birth, the land where, since I had lost my early home, I had found nothing but hard treatment and hunger. No loving ones awaited me there, or anywhere else in the wide world, and it was a matter of absolute certainty that in no case could I expect such generous pay and treatment as I was receiving in Australia. But the impulse would not be resisted, and presently I voluntarily cut myself off from the life of ease and plenty I had been leading by signing articles in a barque bound for home *via* Rangoon.

Physically I was much improved, Australia having been wonderfully kind to me, but spiritually

F

—well, all my early impressions were, if not obliterated, lying so dormant that I did not realise their existence. And although I did not, could not realise it at the time, I was now taking a voyage that would give me an exceedingly dangerous view of Christianity, a view that had never occurred to me before. It may seem a very singular thing to some people, but with all my varied experience packed into a few years I had never up till that time consciously come into contact with a hypocrite. In fact, I did not know what a hypocrite was, except that it was an exceedingly bad kind of character for which the first Gentleman in the world's history had thought no denunciation too severe.

The idea of using religion as a decoy whereby to entrap trustful souls, as a cloak beneath which the safe performance of evil deeds might be indulged in, was a new one entirely to me, but it was now to be revealed to me in all its hideous deformity in the person of my new skipper. I found him behind a public-house bar in Margaret Street, Sydney, looking exactly like some careless publican who had been drinking the profits of his business. He drew me a glass of ale with an air of

proprietorship, his pimply, purple visage all aglow
with recent drinking, and it was there that I
completed my bargain with him. It was very
foolish of me, for a little consideration would have
assured me that such a man was unlikely to be a
good commander to sail under. But I did not
consider, and dearly I paid for my lack of fore-
thought. For upon getting to sea we found that
in order to indulge in his vices he had stinted the
ship of provisions, so that only a few days after
leaving that land of most plentiful and cheap food
we were reduced almost to the verge of starvation,
not only by reason of the scantiness of food, but
because of the exceeding vileness of what little
was served out to us.

And then I learned to my horror that this man
had obtained his present berth on account of his
being an ardent teetotaller and a sincerely devout
Christian. The owners of the ship were men of
the highest probity and prominence in the world
of Christian effort, who spared no pains to make
their ships as comfortable as they could be made,
and took every precaution they could think of in
the selection of their masters in the hope that thus
their ships might be little centres of God's light at

F 2

sea. Some sailors will smile cynically at this, remembering firms of whom the same thing has been often said by interested friends, but whose ships were far worse found and more meanly run than the majority of those owned by firms who made no profession of aims other than purely commercial. I should not quarrel with these critics, because nearly all sailors know of such firms, but in the present case the owners were certainly not to blame. We carried two apprentices, both well-educated and sensible lads, who had begun their sea-life that voyage and were now half-way through their time, the vessel having been absent from home two years when I joined her. And their testimony, although they were smarting under a sense of the grossest injustice in the fact of their parents having been mulcted of a large premium—60*l*. each—for the privilege of their being made scavengers and living worse than hogs, was that the owners had provisioned the ship plentifully and well upon leaving home. They also said that they knew from the skipper's own information to their parents that his orders were to purchase without stint the best food that could be obtained in the colonies.

Yet now I was face to face with the fact that here was a man who had obtained his position by the profession of Christianity, and by the assertion of his desire to hold religious services in the cabin at every opportunity for the benefit of the souls of his crew, who was doing his very best to make the name of the Christian religion stink in the nostrils of all with whom he came in contact. Religion was the topic that most frequently came up for discussion in that vessel's fo'csle, but never a word was said in its favour by anybody. I did not take part in these discussions, partly because of my position as ordinary seaman, which in those days prohibited the holder of it from speaking unless he was spoken to, and partly from a growing feeling that what these men said might be true—that is, that all professors of religion were tarred with the same brush as our old skipper. They agreed among themselves that religion was invented by cunning men for the purpose of keeping themselves on the top of things, eating the fat, drinking the sweet, and clothing themselves with the wool, while the silly sheep who listened to these wily inventors were beguiled into believing that an almighty and all-wise

Being had ordered the world so—had delegated
His power to this gang of plotting marauders.
We had several Bibles in this fo'csle, but they
were very seldom used by anybody. It did not
seem to occur to the debaters to search the
Scriptures, either to see whether their arguments
could be supported by it or the reverse. I looked
into one occasionally, but in a listless, perfunctory
way, for I had access to a good many other books,
and the old sense of task-work still asserted itself
whenever I took up a Bible.

As showing the utter illogicality of the discussions indulged in it was curious to see how, in
spite of the evidence of the apprentices, the owners
were placed upon precisely the same level of condemnation as the skipper. Imaginary offences
were alleged against them, the lightest of which
was that they were in the habit of attending the
sales of condemned naval stores, and having made
a sufficient purchase to victual a couple of ships
for lengthy voyages, would forthwith attend a
prayer meeting and offer up thanksgiving for the
success vouchsafed to their honest efforts in
business. Oh! it was a miserable mole-eyed
business, this constant carping at religion in that

ship's fo'csle, but it was easily explicable, and certainly the responsibility for it lay at the skipper's door.

After a most wretched passage we arrived at Rangoon, where the skipper at once resumed his harbour habit of putting up at some groggery ashore, and remaining there steadily soaking during the vessel's stay in harbour. I do not intend to expend any space in recapitulating the events of that stay in Rangoon. I have done it before rather copiously; but one incident occurred which merits more space than I have previously given to it. It was my meeting with an educated Chinese at the great Rangoon pagoda. I was passing my liberty day, since I had scarcely any money to spend, in a visit to this marvellous place, and having made the round of the various groups of buildings, had brought up in one where worship was proceeding. Here at last I was face to face with the reality of what I had so often read about, ' the heathen in his blindness bowing down to wood and stone.' It gave me a severe shock at first, and then curiosity supervened, and I watched most keenly the course of the proceedings. I saw—indeed, I could not help seeing—that there was nothing of reverence in this worship. Palpably it was just a formal performance of certain posturings and repetition of certain words enjoined by custom or ritual. All mechanical, as certain little actions, by-play during the saying of prayers, made abundantly manifest. And with a curious feeling of disappointment at my heart I recalled the conversations of my shipmates, beginning to feel that after all they might be correct in their views, and that all religions were more or less as much a matter of machinery as this obviously was.

And then a strange thing happened which did me a world of good. While all these thoughts had been passing through my mind, with my eyes fixed upon the movements of the praying 'phoongyees,' I had not noticed the close proximity of a splendidly-dressed Chinaman, who was regarding me with quite as much interest as I was bestowing upon the pseudo-worshippers before me. At last, having seen a favourable opportunity, I suppose, my neighbour accosted me. He said, in purest English without a trace of foreign accent, 'I suppose you do not believe in this form of worship?' I stared up at him in almost stupid amazement, and then having slowly recovered from my surprise, I replied, 'Why, certainly not. How could I? You don't either, I should imagine.' I confess I was not prepared to hear him say, 'Oh yes, this is my religion, but you believe in Jesus Christ, I presume?' Thank God for that question. It swept away as a breath of wind does the deadly fog-wreath settling down upon the sea and making navigation full of peril, the miasmatic mists of unbelief that recent experience had caused to settle down upon my mind. It gave me an opportunity of stating my position as far as I knew it, gave me, too, an exalted sense of being able to bear witness to the truth of God in the person of His Son. Even out of the thick darkness of my ignorance this light flooded my soul, and I answered brightly, long-forgotten lessons coming sharply and clearly into my memory, 'Yes, I believe in Jesus Christ. He came to teach us the love of God for man, and to show us that the way to happiness here and after death was a plain and straight one. He Himself was, and is, the Way; He lived among men doing kindness to all, and at last, misunderstood, ill-treated, and broken-hearted, He was put to death.

And although He could easily have got away and left us all to ourselves, He did not, but died as a sacrifice for our sins, the last sacrifice, rightly so called, that there ever was in the world. And He waits now up there,' and I pointed above my head, 'to receive all those who have honoured Him by believing His words.'

Panting with eagerness, full of wonder at myself for the energy with which I had been pressing the claims of God—claims that I thought of so little that I fancied them forgotten—I paused, looking up into that sphinx-like face. Not a shade of expression upon it, no gleam of interest, and I felt much as I should imagine one would feel upon suddenly discovering that he had been addressing a stone-deaf man or a waxen effigy which he had mistaken for a living person. Then the colourless lips opened and he spoke :

'When I was at Cambridge reading for my degree,' he said, 'the subject of religion had a peculiar fascination for me. We Easterns are invariably of a metaphysical turn of mind, and problems arise in our discussion of theories intricate and far-reaching to an extent of which you Western races can form no estimate. So for a long time,

as a mental recreation, I unravelled the threads
spun by religionists of the West, finding as I went
on less and less difficulty in understanding them,
but led off into recondite speculations whereof the
authors whose works I was studying never even
dreamed. It was most enjoyable, but most un-
profitable also from the point of view of the business for which I was in your country. Therefore
since we Chinese are also an exceedingly practical race, I had no hesitation whatever in aban-
doning my speculative researches into religion,
which was, after all, only an intellectual amusement, and resuming my old mental attitude
towards all religion. This is, that so vast a subject is only for the few who are able to devote to
it the study of a lifetime. For the many, it is
enough that they receive as much instruction as is
fitting for them at the hands of the priests, perform the ordered ceremonies, pay the demanded
cost, and trouble their heads about the why of
the matter nothing at all. After all, who am I
that I should presume to be wiser than the
myriads of my ancestors who lived and died in
this faith? It sufficed them, and the thin skin of
Western varnish that I have received does not make

me consider myself wiser or better in any way than those revered ones who have preceded me.'

He ceased, and I leave it to my readers to imagine what effect his beautiful voice, his smoothly-flowing periods, and his, to my awe-struck mind, supernal wisdom had upon me with my abysmal ignorance and uncultured manners. In the first place, I felt dirty, rough, and awkward. In the next, I could find no words to answer him, although I longed, oh, how I longed! to say some-thing that might convince him of the superiority of the God whom I worshipped, however feebly, over all the world-elected gods. But the odds were too great. Beside that cultivated pagan I was as ill at ease as if I had been in the presence of a king, and I made haste to take leave of him, glad enough to escape.

I returned on board my ship considerably dis-concerted, and that night began to read the Bible with an interest I never before felt. I confess that my interest flagged soon, but fortunately for me the other books on board were fairly ex-hausted. So I began a practice, which I con-tinued as long as I was at sea, viz. the reading of a chapter or two on turning in every watch below

if there was light enough to see the words. Not
with any idea of 'being good' or of obtaining
spiritual benefit, but for information solely. I
had an earnest desire to learn what I felt the
Bible alone could teach, so that in case I should
again meet a foreigner trained in England who
should ask me such a question as the Chinaman
did I should not look quite so foolish.

Why should I linger over the sordid, miserable
details of that passage to England? With the
crew absolutely out of hand in consequence of the
skipper's disgusting behaviour, it was only some
lingering compunction in their minds that kept
them obedient to the two mates, who were much
liked. The sailors abused the master to his face
whenever he dared to give an order or attempted
in any way to show his authority. It was the
only way they had of showing their resentment at
the long months of starvation which we needlessly
endured on the passage home. At last it dragged
lingeringly to a close, and we found ourselves
anchored at Gravesend. A gentle-faced missionary came on board to talk to the crew, and having
first obtained permission from the officers, he
stepped forward to the fo'csle. The sight of his

clerical garb—he was a Churchman—acted upon the fellows as a red flag is said to do upon a bull, but although they said some horrible things before he came within hearing, no sooner had he, lifting his hat, asked permission to enter our gloomy abode than they were all dumb. It was a most painful situation for him, coming upon an errand of mercy to be met with speechless anger.

As the voyage was practically ended, I made bold to break the fo'csle etiquette for once, which forbade an ordinary seaman to speak while his superiors were silent, and addressing him respectfully, I said : 'I'm afraid, sir, you wonder at your reception, but with your permission I will explain matters a little. This vessel is owned by a firm notorious for their profession of religion, and we are told that one member of the firm preaches every Sunday. The skipper was chosen to command because he professed to be a Christian and a teetotaller, so that she is what you might call a holy ship. Yet during the whole voyage the skipper has, whenever possible, been drunk ; he was notorious in every port the vessel has called at for his lecherous behaviour, and his attempts to swindle public-house keepers and others of the same class. Through this conduct of his we have been reduced to skin and bone, as you see, and, rightly or wrongly, but quite excusably, I think, we've considered skipper and owners as beastly hypocrites altogether. Look at this, sir!' and as I spoke I laid before him a mess-kid—a small tub —in which lay a piece of something that looked exactly like a lump of dirty white salt. 'Do you know what this is, sir?' I inquired. He looked at it earnestly for some time before answering, then said, reluctantly I thought, 'No, I confess I do not know what it can be. Some curious mineral, perhaps.' 'No, sir,' I rejoined triumphantly, 'that is the allowance of beef for five men for one day, yesterday, and to show you that I am not imposing upon you'—here I broke off a piece and showed him the grain of the meat and the bone within. Then taking a fragment in my hands I rubbed it into a fine powder, so absolutely without succulence or nourishment had it become. Then I showed him some biscuit, which, lightly tapped upon the deck, fell into a little heap of grey rubbish, crawling with vermin.

That good man's face was a study. He looked sick, disgusted, disheartened. 'You are not surprised now, are you, sir, that the men do not look upon you as a minister of religion with favour ? A long course of this treatment, which they believe to have been meted out to them under cover of religion, has made them feel revengefully towards all professors of religion whatever.' Sadly he answered : ' No, I cannot say that 1 am. But I am so sorry, so sorry ! I can only go—and pray for you all, hoping that you will learn that for the wickedness of wolves in sheep's clothing God is not to blame. Good-bye, men, and God bless you ! '

So he went, and I looked after him with a feeling that he had been very badly treated for what he was powerless to help. But I have often thought since that he was too easily discouraged. He might have tried to explain the difference between professors of religion and Christians. I feel sure that a little genial talk would have broken down the sullen reserve of my shipmates, and perhaps made them feel that there might be, after all, some real followers of the Man who went about doing good.

I spent about three weeks in London enjoying myself in rational fashion, that is to say, I lived on good food, drank little, read a great deal, and visited all the sights of London. Then, before my money was all gone, I got another ship as ordinary seaman, the fine clipper 'Rangitiki,' bound to Port Chalmers, New Zealand. How my heart thrills as I write the name of that place, to me the dearest spot upon the whole earth's surface. But I must not anticipate.

We carried a fairly large number of passengers and a pretty good crew, but two-thirds of them were paralysed with drink when they came on board, and before they were fit for duty we were out in mid-channel in mid-winter, struggling with the handiwork of riggers who did not care what became of the ship once she was out of their sight. A whole chapter might be written in the most lurid terms, that should nevertheless not be in the least exaggerated, of the miseries of such a beginning to a voyage. Only those who have been through it can form any idea of its horror, when in the grip of a winter gale, in imminent danger of collision, a half-dead crew are struggling vainly with half-bent sails and wrongly-rove gear through the long hours of a terrible night. But under such circumstances men go about their work in mechanical fashion, dumbly enduring pain and cold

G

and the extremity of toil, and when once the strain is over they forget it all like children. But, oh, the danger of it!

This, too, was a Godless ship, as far as any recognition by the powers aft of any religious duties went. But for me she was a blessed craft indeed. As I have before hinted, I was now a pretty rough character, strong and hearty, and living for what little pleasure I could get out of life. To my mind the world was inhabited by selfish people who never did a kind action but with an eye to profit, and as to religion, well, there *might* be something in it; but as far as my experience went, it was all veneer for money-making purposes. So low had I sunk. Now on board of this vessel there was a lank, swarthy lad of about my own age, who from his awkwardness, his uselessness, and his extremely comical appearance was the butt of all hands, but especially of the very wicked apprentices with whom he lived. He suffered agonies in sea-sickness for nearly three weeks, and I, who have never quite got the upper hand of that sea-scourge, was very sympathetic towards him. He was a lad of good family, who was, although nominally an ordinary seaman, really taking the voyage for the benefit of his health. And when he became convalescent, being in the same watch as myself, we chummed up, and through the long night watches in fine weather we talked incessantly.

He had been a postulant in Llanthony Abbey, a born mystic, who in ancient days would have worn the martyr's crown with great joy. His health, however, failed under the tremendous mental strain, and he was obliged to abandon the monastic idea. He was, besides, an artist, a passionate lover of poetry, a great reader, and a gentleman to his finger tips. And in return for such small material help as I had been able to give him, he poured out upon me the riches with which his mind was stored. He spoke of Father Ignatius, so lovingly, so tenderly; of the solemn round of life in the Abbey, of the inner mysteries of the Christian faith as cherished in monkish bosoms. Then he plied me with poetry—even now I fancy I can see him in the gloom under the break of the poop, declaiming in a strenuous whisper long passages from the 'Golden Legend' and the 'Idylls of the King.' Only in this way was he able to overcome my ignorant hatred of

G 2

poetry, and change it as he did into the most passionate admiration. Then he fought down my cynical opinion of friendship, telling me story after story out of his own experience about the faithfulness of friends, their disinterestedness, their unwearied clinging to those whom they had befriended, as if they were under the obligation themselves.

Yet in all these long talks, although I was soaking up knowledge like a sponge, there was never a single word of spiritual import, never a hint of our jointly approaching the Father and following in the footsteps of His Son. It was all external religion, external beauty, for which, perhaps, the natural shyness of English lads was to blame. But the time when all that should be altered was close at hand.

CHAPTER V

THE DAWN

WE reached our port after a very rapid passage, and at once proceeded to our moorings at Port Chalmers Wharf. Being by this time very well accustomed to strange sights, I was in no wise impressed by the pretty little town beyond noting that it *was* pretty and that the surrounding country was exceedingly picturesque. A ship's first day in a foreign port is usually a busy time for the sailors getting her into harbour-trim—that is, unbending sails, stripping off chafing gear, neatly fastening up the coils of running rigging, &c. Therefore none of us had much leisure for looking around until work was done for the day, and then it was dark. Nevertheless, we all noticed that nestling under the side of a huge hill that overlooked the wharves were several buildings, conspicuous among them being a square warehouse-looking erection of three floors, and, a little to the right of it, a much more ornate building, also of three floors, bearing the legend, ' Port Hotel.' As these conspicuous houses lay right at the end of the pier at which we were moored, they naturally attracted our attention first.

When evening came and, released from labour, we strolled ' up town,' we speedily found that the little port was not without attractions specially designed for seamen. One of these soon claimed me, for I heard singing, an attraction I was never able to resist if I could, by any means, gain admittance to where it was going on. In this case admittance was free. A large room at the back of a ' hotel '—all public-houses are hotels in Australia and New Zealand—plainly furnished with benches and tables, with a platform and a piano, was set apart as a ' free and easy,' to which all were welcomed as potential purchasers of drink. The place was respectable and well-conducted, no rowdyism of any kind being allowed. ' Any gentleman willing to oblige ' stepped up on to the platform, sang his song, and retired, and to keep matters going, the landlord himself mounted the platform at intervals and obliged, being applauded uproariously, despite the undoubted poverty of his performance. Drunkenness was not permitted on the premises, and if, as sometimes happened, a toper took sufficient away with him in a bottle to complete his fuddlement, Nemesis usually overtook him in the shape of a particularly vigilant constable, and severe punishment invariably followed, for drunkenness and vagrancy were by no means venial offences in New Zealand.

So, in the course of the first week, I became a regular attendant at the sing-song, where for sixpence one might spend an hour or two pleasantly enough away from the ship's gloomy fo'csle. Then came Sunday, when not feeling sufficiently fine in dress to go ashore among the neatly-clad population, two or three of us borrowed a boat and went fishing until dark. After supper (six P.M.) someone suggested that we should go up to the hotel where the sing-song was held, for, although the Sunday Closing Act was in force, we should be sure to find the back door open, and we could go in, get a drink, and meet our friends. Agreed, we would go. Accordingly my shipmate and myself were soon strolling along the pier townwards with that leisurely swagger peculiar to sailors, and had reached the open space in front of the warehouse before mentioned, when a burst of melody floating overhead on the evening air brought me up all standing. It was so sweet, so unearthly, that all sorts of queer sensations chased one another over my body, and when my companion said, 'Come along,' I waved him off with an impatient gesture. I could not bear to be interrupted in my exquisite enjoyment of those celestial sounds. They ceased, and my chum said quietly, 'I know what it is ; it's a meetin'. I ben to 'em before. Let's go in.' 'Not me,' I answered. 'I don't go shoving my nose where it isn't wanted. Maybe it's a few friends having a few hymns for their own pleasure on a Sunday night.' But even while I spoke I was filled with a deep longing to get nearer to that lovely music, although failing any possibility of that I would have been well content to stand just where I was until midnight. So fond was I of music that I have often in Sydney given the last sixpence I had to street musicians whose performances were specially to my liking.

While I stood anxiously waiting for the music to begin again, my companion murmured, 'Hold on a bit. I'll go and see if we can get in,' and hurried towards the building. In a few minutes

he returned triumphantly, saying, ' I told ye so ;
they begged me to call you in, sayin' that we was
hearty welcome ; it was got up for the like of us.'
' All right, go ahead,' I replied, more gratified than
I could express, but I was somewhat surprised still
to find such an affair under way in a warehouse.
We climbed a steep and tortuous series of stairs
to the top of the building, where a sweet-faced
little man with fair whiskers met us, and, giving us
books, conducted us to a seat among the benches
a few rows from the platform. As soon as he had
left us I looked wonderingly around, for I had
never been in such a place before. It was a sail-
loft, an immense bare room with naked rafters
overhead and brick walls just whitewashed. The
seats were rough wooden forms, with the exception of a few chairs on the platform, where was
also a small table. Gathered close to the platform
was a little company of well-dressed men and
women intent upon the words of a thick-set, dark-
visaged man, who was addressing them volubly,
with a book in his hand. Suddenly I heard him
say, ' Now then, one, two,' and with a sweep of his
arm he launched them into another burst of song,
quite unaccompanied, but wonderfully sweet.

I sat spellbound. What with my unfamiliar surroundings, the delightful sounds, and my wonder at what would come next, the time flew past so rapidly that although we were almost the first arrivals and the preliminary singing lasted an hour we did not appear to have been there more than five minutes before there was an expectant hush. Three gentlemen, including the dark little choir leader, mounted the platform, and the latter, stepping forward, said, 'Friends, we will commence our meeting to-night by singing with all our hearts that beautiful prayer, " Jesu, lover of my soul," number —— in the books you have. And will you all remember that it is a prayer ? Although written in rhyme and sung to music, it is as much a prayer as " Our Father," and I hope that all who sing it will not for one moment allow the fact to be forgotten. So will you certainly be blessed in your singing.'

I listened eagerly, reverently, but when the large audience which had now gathered rose to their feet, and at the signal from the leader the choir burst into the opening bars of ' Hollingside,' I was reduced to blind dumbness. The pent-up feelings of years broke loose, scalding tears ran down, and something stuck in my throat like a ball. I knew that tune so well, and I had not heard it sung since those happy days in the Old Lock Chapel, which seemed to belong to another life. But by a strong effort I recovered my composure, and then, how I did sing ! I just abandoned myself to an ecstasy of pure joy.

The singing ceased and we sat down. Then a gentleman on the platform prayed. He offered up a prayer that, allowing for the different diction, sent my mind flying back to poor black Jem of the ' Arabella.' For it was a prayer, not a formula. The utterer, while deeply reverent as became one in the secret chamber of the King's House, was also quietly confident. And he did not do that evil thing that I have so often heard done since— preach at his audience under pretence of praying to God. Just as a child asks its mother for food, so he asked God for definite recognition of the efforts of his friends and himself for the benefit of those present, especially the sailors.

Just here I would like to repeat that while to so many of my readers the above description is but an exact record of facts, perhaps the best known of their lives, to me all that was going on was absolutely novel. Never before in my life had I been in such a place or heard such a service as this. May I then be forgiven for minutely recording my impressions, bearing in mind the infinite importance, to me, of the whole affair?

The prayer ended, we sang another hymn—surely, I thought, there was never such a beautiful collection of hymns as this one—and after the hymn, the little dark choir-leader produced his Bible and read the first chapter of Isaiah. As I listened, I got an idea of the exquisiteness of perfect prose. For the reader was not only a scholar, but a splendid reader, who read the Bible as if it were a living message to living men thirsting for it, and not as if the understanding of it were the last thing necessary, the fact of it having been gabbled or muttered or intoned over, however unintelligibly, being the main point. I suppose that in the whole of our splendid literature there is no book that is so shamefully treated by being read aloud as is the Bible. Why, I do not know, but the fact remains. I have heard men of the highest scholarly attainments read the Bible so vilely that my face has burned with indignation as I thought of the unpardonable waste of opportunity, especially knowing that the same men would have perfectly declaimed a page of Shakespeare.

Then more singing, I could not get enough of that—followed by another novelty to me, a solo from the choir-leader, 'The Ninety and Nine.' Oh, what pathos, what a depth of yearning love for the souls of men he did impart to that simple little poem with its bald tune! I could have melted in tears, but with tightly-shut lips and hardly breathing, I managed to maintain control of myself. Then one of the two other gentlemen spoke, quite nicely, I thought, but not sufficiently clear and direct to hold my attention. Full of earnestness, full of kindly intention, but so discursive and disconnected that I found my thoughts wandering sadly, and, had the service ended with that address, I should not now be writing these words. For the novelty was wearing off, and I was becoming critical. But before this deadening process had gone on too long, the speaker ceased his address, and another hymn was sung. At its close the energetic leader of the choir, who had charmed me so much by his reading, advanced to the verge of the platform and began to speak. I was all attention now, for the Gospel was being unfolded in all its simplicity and directness. I felt as if there was only one person there for whom those words were meant—me. I listened with all my soul, every syllable coming with such force to my heart and understanding as I have never since heard. There were no tricks of oratory, no declamation, no attempt to frighten ; indeed, it was a tender appeal from a heart overflowing with loving desire to help a fellow wayfarer out of darkness into the Lightened Way of Life.

I do not know how long the address lasted. I only knew that something was being offered to me that I felt I must have. I felt like one who after long wandering in a gloomy labyrinth, so long that he had grown to accept the gloom and the maze as the settled conditions of his life, from which there was no hope of escape, had suddenly seen open before him a door leading into sunlighted meadows with a delightful prospect stretching beyond into infinity. Any words, however, can only feebly express the intense longing of my being, for an experience of this personal, loving acquaintance with the sympathetic man Christ Jesus, so earnestly set forth by the speaker. And yet, when at the close of his address he invited all who were moved to seek the Lord to stay behind for further consideration of the matter, while those who wished to leave were departing, I was filled with a torturing shyness. Had my chum, whose existence I had forgotten until that moment, although he was sitting by my side, risen and said, 'Come along,' I fear I should have gone. But to my unspeakable relief, instead of doing that he leaned towards me whispering, 'I sh'd like to stop, ole man.' 'So sh'd I,' I replied eagerly, and together we waited while the choir sang away, and the audience thinned out until there were only about a dozen anxious ones scattered over the waste of empty benches.

Presently all was quiet, and I sat with my face buried in my hands just waiting for—I knew not what. My mind was a confused whirl of thoughts, out of which nothing definite emerged but that deep sense of heart-hunger. While I thus sat in painful expectation of the performance of some miracle a hand was gently laid upon my shoulder. Looking up, I saw a man whom I had not noticed before. He sat down by my side and began to ask me questions, such as, 'Did I want to be saved? What was my difficulty? Why did I not come to the Lord now?' and so on, questions which I felt utterly incapable of answering. I did not know what I wanted—I did not know anything, except that I was trembling with eager anticipation of a possible blessed setting free from a life I hated, and being placed in intimate relationship with this intensely lovable personal Friend of whom I had been hearing. I am afraid my interlocutor was a little disgusted at what he not unnaturally took to be utter stupidity, for with a little sharpness in his voice, instantly noted and resented by me, he began to catechise me as to the conditions of the Christian faith. Here I was at home, my mind cleared at once, and I not only answered his questions easily, but put others to him which surprised him. At last he said, 'Well, if you know these things, you must be saved. I don't see where your difficulty lies.' 'Neither do I,' I replied; 'but although I have known these things, as you say, ever since I was old enough to think, that knowledge hasn't kept me from being miserable, hasn't kept me from the fear of being damned.'

A few more words passed between us, and then he left me with a discontented look upon his face. But I cannot hope to give any idea of the miserable state of mind I was now in. It seemed to me as if the gates of a goodly city of which I, so long an outcast, should be an honoured freeman, had just been opened far enough to give me a comprehensive view of the glories within, and then, as I was about to enter, those portals had closed against me, shutting me out again into the dark desert of despair, lonely beyond all telling. I do not say that my feelings could have been as definitely stated then; indeed, I am sure they could not, because I know that I was as one who has received a mortal wound, whose nerve-centres refuse to perform their office of intelligently distributing his sensations.

While in this sad frame, oblivious of all that was passing around me, another hand touched me. Now, it may seem difficult to believe, but I declare that the touch of that hand gave me a thrill of hope. Why, I do not profess to explain, but the fact I know and record gratefully. Looking up, I saw the face of the dark little man who had so moved me by his earnest commendation to his

H

hearers of the brother-love of the sorrowful Man. Meeting my dim, stupid gaze with a look full of sympathy, he held out his hand, and when I took it he did not let it go, but drew himself down by it, as it were, to a seat by my side.

'My dear boy,' he said, 'I am not going to ask you what your difficulties are. I have no right to do so, but I am going to tell you that He who has removed mine is ready to remove yours. Ready, yes, and eager to take that despairing look from your eyes, to show you the delights of His unchangeable love. Listen, " He that believeth on Me, though he were dead, yet shall he live, and he that liveth and believeth on Me shall never die. Believest thou this ? " ' As he looked inquiringly I replied, 'Yes, I believe ; I dare not say I do not believe. I have always believed, even when through hearing my shipmates denying His existence, I have been tempted to agree with them.' 'Then you have entered upon everlasting life,' he said triumphantly. I sorrowfully shook my head, saying, 'Oh, no, I cannot, I dare not say that ; it wouldn't be true ! I haven't the slightest feeling of the kind, and it would be a lie to say that I have.' 'Oh, I see !' he answered. 'Very well, then let me put a case. Supposing that you were worrying dreadfully about a debt which you could not pay. You know me as a very wealthy man, who is not only fond of doing kind deeds, but whose trustworthiness is beyond suspicion. It comes to my knowledge that you are in trouble, and I tell you that I have paid your debt. You say that you believe me because you feel that I deserve to be believed ; you profess entire faith in me, but you still go on worrying about that debt. Instead of going about with a light heart rejoicing in your freedom, you are bowed down with care. Would that not prove that you did not really believe what I said, but that you were waiting for some other proof of my truth to produce the feeling of safety you longed for ? '

'Yes, it would,' I replied. 'Well, then listen to me, or, rather, listen to Jesus : "He that believeth on Me *hath* everlasting life, and shall *not* come into condemnation, but *is passed* from death unto life." Do you believe this ? ' 'Yes,' I whispered. 'Then you have passed from death unto life, you are in the timeless state of eternal life, are you not ? ' 'No,' I answered doggedly. 'Ah, I see how it is, friend. You are waiting for the witness of your feelings to the truth of Him who is *the* Truth. You dare not take Him at His word unless your feelings, which are subject to a thousand changes a day, corroborate it. Do believe Him, in spite of your feelings, and act accordingly.'

Every word spoken by the earnest little man went right to my heart, and when he ceased there was an appeal in his eyes that was even more eloquent than his words. But beyond the words and the look was the interpretation of them to me by some mysterious agency beyond all my com- prehension. For in a moment the hidden mystery was made clear to me, and I said quietly, 'I see, sir ; it is the credibility of God against the witness of my feelings. Then I believe God.' 'Let us thank God,' answered the little man, and together we knelt down by the bench.

Little more was said, wisely on his part, because although that which I so sorely needed was now mine, I was only able to grasp one idea at a time ; all the rest of my mind was still numbed. There was no extravagant joy, no glorious bursting into light and liberty such as I have since read about as happening on those occasions ; it was just a lesson learned—the satisfaction consequent upon finding one's way after long groping in darkness and misery—a way that led to peace.

I love that description of conversion as the 'new birth.' No other definition touches the truth of the process at all. So helpless, so utterly knowledgeless, possessing nothing but the consciousness of Life just begun is the new-born Christian. For this reason I have always mistrusted frantic demonstrations of joy in those professing to have just entered into Life. Happiness there certainly is, but it is the happiness of one who after long delirium of fever awakes one morning with cool hands and head, a delicious sensation of restfulness pervading every nerve, a consciousness of serene enjoyment of the dawn smiling in through the window, of the fresh cleanliness of the room, of healthy hunger presently to be satisfied.

But I had forgotten my chum for the time. My first impulse upon the settlement of the great question was to tell him, so I turned eagerly to where he had been sitting, meeting his bright face as full of satisfaction as my own. He told me, however, that his joy arose from the fact that he had returned after a time of backsliding—that he had been converted two years before, but had wandered away, and oh, how glad he was to get back! We exchanged confidences with childish eagerness, full of affectionate interest in each other, until I said, 'Well, I suppose we must be going, although I feel as if I should like to stay here. I dread going back to the ship.' And then a sudden thought seized me, and I whispered, 'I should like to die now.' I did not then know how old that feeling was, the feeling of the demoniac when his devils had been cast out that he must forsake all and follow Jesus, although the Master bids him return and be a missionary to his own people.

So we quietly rose to depart, and had reached the top of the stairs when one of the choir came running after us and bade us welcome to somebody's house for a little refreshment. Gladly and gratefully we went with the party to a very nice house, whose beautiful furniture and air of comfort was a revelation to me. I had never been in such a place before since I was old enough to notice it. There we were pleasantly fed and entertained with conversation and singing, and when at last the party broke up we felt that we had made quite a large circle of friends, each one of whom would be glad to see us at any reasonable time and do his or her best to make us feel at home.

We said little to each other as we returned on board, only 'Good night and God bless you!' as my chum went to his berth and I sought mine. To my great relief the fo'csle was quite quiet—all hands were asleep. So I knelt down by a chest and thanked God for His Fatherly care and love in bringing me to this place and permitting me to find these people. I did not ask for anything; I was full of thanksgiving for benefits received. And immediately I got into my bed, miserable heap of straw though it was, I fell sound asleep, as befitted one from whose mind every care had flown.

Returning to work next morning, I was surprised to find how easily everything went. Orders had been given to clean and paint the ship inside and out, and at a job like this, with energetic officers, a great deal of hard work is done with its usual concomitant of blasphemous growling. But I had no desire to growl. It seemed the easiest thing in the world to be willing and obedient, to do everything that was given me to do with the utmost care, and endeavour to make the job as perfect as I was able. Then when breakfast time came, after carrying in the food, instead of rushing upon my share, I felt inclined to wash, a thing which excited several derisive remarks at so unusual a proceeding. I felt myself a quiet wonder at this impulse, but obeyed it, sitting down afterwards to my unsavoury meal with a fervent 'thank God,' another impulse for which I could not account.

The day wore to a close in this strange fashion. Generally very fond of chat, I seemed to-day only anxious to enjoy the soundless peace within, not attempting to analyse its reasons. In the midst of all the turmoil about me I felt as one feels who loves Nature and finds himself on a perfect June morning lying alone on a lonely hillside in Surrey, with the returning life of the land bidding his heart rejoice in the unspoken language of Infinite Love. Or at the dayspring in the tropics when the plain of ocean lies, like the Apocalyptic sea, under the first kiss of the sun, the sails hang motionless in windless silence, and the universe is sensibly sur-charged with the peace of God. But all similes fail to suggest truly the rest-time of the soul when it has for the first time heard the loving voice of the All-Father, and has found that instead of coming to an awful judgment-seat, overshadowed by the terrible frown of an offended Jehovah, it is welcomed by the still small Voice of a Father yearning over wandering ones, by the enfolding arms of the Nazarene Carpenter, whose contact conveys perfect life and peace and joy beyond all thought.

Also I found that for the first time for several years I had not used a single oath all day. And I remembered the many occasions when I had, with many tears, bound myself with the strongest vows possible to cease from swearing, and had always failed lamentably. Yet to-day, without an effort on my part, without giving the matter a moment's thought, I had found my tongue holden. No sooner had work ceased, and my service to my shipmates was done, than I dressed and hurried ashore for more communion with those to whom I felt I owed so much. I found only one of them, no meeting being held, but that one, although he was busy at his trade of a barber, received me with such a beaming smile of welcome that I felt my lip quivering like a baby's. Coming on top of the day's experience, that look of loving welcome was almost more than my softened heart could bear.

CHAPTER VI

NEW SAILING ORDERS

AMID all the scrubbing, painting, and polishing that went on during that week, a rumour steadily gained ground amongst us that, owing to the Master's leaving, all hands would be discharged. Now all sailors look upon this proceeding as their right, although the articles expressly stipulate that the crew shall serve under 'the said Master or anyone who shall lawfully succeed him.' Whether it be general I do not know, but on this occasion the sailors' wishes were yielded to, and on the completion of the work all who wished to leave the ship were paid off—that is to say, everybody left her except the apprentices. I should have left her, given the opportunity, in any case, having all a merchant seamen's love of change for one thing, and because wages in this place were nearly double what we were then receiving.

But under the new conditions which had befallen me, I looked upon the permission to leave the ship as a direct answer to my prayer to be taken out of the sea-life altogether. I felt terrified at the idea of having to go again to sea and live in the midst of the blasphemy, obscenity, and squalor of the fo'csle. For all on a sudden my taste, my desires, had changed, and that so completely, that I loathed the conditions under which I had been earning my living. I declare that I felt as one would feel, I imagine, who had been accustomed to live in all the refinement and comfort of a wealthy home from birth, and was now suddenly face to face with the prospect of life in a ship's fo'csle, with the added disadvantage of knowing exactly what was in store for him. I do not profess to explain or defend this attitude of mind, or say that it was a necessary adjunct to the new life of the soul, but I know that it was there, and would not be put away.

I mentioned my longings to my new friends, who were all full of kindness, and I know did all in their power to assist me. I applied for various situations, highly recommended by these Christian men, but as soon as I came to be examined as to my qualifications, my hopes were all dashed. My

one accomplishment outside the ordinary work of
a seaman—a love of reading—was utterly valueless.   I could hardly write so as to be readable, I
could not cast up a column of figures.   In short,
I was only fit to be a day labourer.   At last I got
work upon a farm with a Christian family, but my
utter ignorance of farm work made it impossible
for me to earn any pay beyond my food, and I
was soon disheartened at doing that.   Moreover,
the farm was far away from all my friends, and I
wanted to be near them, to learn all that they
could teach me of the Way of Life.

So it came about that I was driven by the
inevitable force of circumstances back to the sea
again, my only comfort being that tendered me
by the dear little barber.   He pointed out to me
how great a dearth of Christians there was on
board ship, what a scope was there afforded for
living the Gospel and spreading the Light.   He
weighted his arguments by the story of the healed
demoniac who pleaded for permission to follow
Jesus, but was bidden to return to his own people
and his own country, and there tell what great
things the Lord had done for him.

And now, for reasons that seem sufficient to

me, principally because I do not desire to go over
the same ground too much, and secondly because
the present seems to be a pleasant opportunity to
gratify the hundreds of friends all over the world
who have written asking for more details of my
life after leaving the 'Cachalot,' I propose to take
a great stride forward. It may be well to state in
so doing that my spiritual development was very
slow, happily for me, throughout that time. I
read my Bible continually, not only for the heart-
food it contained, but with keenest delight; for my
poetry lessons on board the 'Rangitiki' had been so
far entirely profitable in that they had shown me
that the Bible was nearly all poetry. This discovery was followed up by purchase at an old
book-shop of a Paragraph Bible, wherein the baffling
divisions of the Book into chapters and verses had
been done away with, and wherever the words
were metrical, they were so arranged.

In all my reading I do not remember anything
that has afforded me such delight as this discovery
did. From henceforth the Bible was full of music,
and to this day I always associate the reading of
Job or Isaiah with the cadences of a great organ,
or the chanting of thousands of white-robed priests

at the dedication of the Temple. For this delight of insight and appreciation I was, of course, indebted to my enthusiastic friend on board the 'Rangitiki,' about whom I would dearly like to say very much, but that his story belongs to himself, and I am not without hope that he will some day give it to the world. The other young friend, who sat by my side upon that ever-to-be-remembered night in the sail-loft at Port Chalmers, shipped almost immediately after leaving the 'Rangitiki,' and I never saw or heard of him again.

Once more, to my great delight, after a long, long absence, I found myself at Port Chalmers, no longer a boy, but a young man, fit and confident or his life-work, whatever that might be. I did not yet feel reconciled to the sea as a means of livelihood, but was fast becoming aware that, for a long time to come, I should be of no use in any situation ashore that I could think of. My friends in Port Chalmers had not only not forgotten me, they welcomed me with a warmth that was deeply affecting. Let me say here that in all my experience among them I never found one that tried to make of me a proselyte to his particular denomination. I know, of course, that there are many most estimable and lovable Christians who hate the word 'undenominational' most heartily —in their minds it is almost, if not quite, a synonym for unchristian. To my mind, this attitude is a most painful and disheartening one. In all secular affairs it is recognised that one absolute essential to success in any undertaking is that all those who have its interests at heart shall pull together, be of one mind, as far as its fortunes are concerned. Why, then, should Christianity be, as Drummond so wisely called it, 'The Great Exception'? Even the most mole-eyed controversialist must acknowledge the loss of power involved in the friction arising over differences in non-essentials.

Perhaps, however, this is a little out of my line. It arises from my recollection of the manner in which the Baptists, the Wesleyans, the Presbyterians, the Brethren, and the Episcopalians in Port Chalmers at that time tacitly agreed to sink all minor differences in their combined onslaught upon the common enemy. And we poor sailors who were gathered in there were never allowed to feel for one moment that there was any jealousy between the different bodies, or that it mattered

one pin's-point whither we went to worship. There
had been one exception to this good rule, beside
the Romish communion—which, of course, could
not allow any of her sons to work with heretics—
the Episcopalian. But that was speedily altered
by the coming of a new incumbent, the Rev.
Lorenzo Moore, who at once in the heartiest
manner announced his intention of assisting in
the mission work among seamen, and proved a
most valuable helper.

I went to his church when I discovered this,
and although it would be impossible for me to
explain how delighted I felt at the new meaning
all those beautiful prayers now had for me, I can
say that my visit gave me a restful sense of having
returned home. The preacher announced at that
service an approaching confirmation, and carefully
explained the significance of the rite. This set
me thinking. Was it not necessary that I should
relieve my sponsors of their obligations, even though
it was probably true that they themselves had
never realised them? Deciding that it was, I
seized the first opportunity afforded me of calling
upon Mr. Moore and asking if I might be admitted.
He received me most lovingly, and when my

errand was hesitatingly explained he laid his hand paternally on my shoulder, saying, 'Do you think that being confirmed will make you any better, or will add any certainty to your salvation?' Without a moment's hesitation I answered, 'No; I only wanted to relieve my sponsors of their vows.'

'In that case,' he replied, 'I bid you heartily welcome; but had you been under the impression that any outside application was necessary to your salvation, or that anything but a change of heart was of real importance in the sight of our Father, I should have refused.' Then we had a long and delightful talk, at the end of which he told me that I need attend none of the classes, as he was assured that my knowledge of the required conditions was far nearer perfection than any candidate he had ever examined. So, in due time, I was confirmed by, I think, the Bishop of Dunedin, and feeling satisfied that I at any rate had done my duty, dismissed the matter from my mind.

Next Sunday I came to the Lord's Table, trembling like one in an ague fit with contending emotions, but never for one instant imagining that the bread and wine were anything but symbols— a sort of commemoration meal, taken in obedience

I

to the wish of the Man Christ Jesus that His friends should remember His loving work on earth for them and its apparently hopeless but really triumphant end. It was several years before I broke bread in a church again.

On this second visit I renewed my eager efforts to obtain work ashore, but all in vain. In fact, had it not been for the ungrudging hospitality of my friends ashore I must have left the port long before I did, as I was penniless. But although I was really, as the Scotch say, 'sorning' on those dear people, and I often wonder how I had the face to do it so long, the experience was invaluable. The refinement of those pleasant homes, the constant rubbing against gentle, cultured people, aided by a certain imitative faculty that I have always possessed, was doing wonders for me in an educational way. I was being taught manners, conversation, getting polished, in fact, until I no longer felt ill at ease or clumsy in decent society.

I was now twenty-one years of age and an able seaman, fit to do anything required of me in such a position. And reluctantly I made up my mind that, as I could not escape from the sea life, I must try and better my position. Priggishness is

hateful, and I dread the accusation of it keenly;
but it is only the bare truth to say that every day
I spent ashore among those kind friends made me
more and more reluctant to go back to the life in
a ship's fo'csle, for I knew so well what to expect.
It was the only point on which I felt unable to
agree with the energetic little Christian man
who had been instrumental in my conversion.
Quoting from Scripture, he laid it down that
every man should abide in the calling wherein he
was abiding when the Lord called him, unless that
calling was an evil one. I felt that he might be
right, but that I could not feel that it was wrong
to wish to change my calling.

However, the choice was denied me. I could
not for very shame's sake linger ashore after it
was manifest that I was unfit for anything that
offered itself, so I got a ship—a large iron vessel,
belonging to Greenock—which was loading for
home. I obtained leave to work on board until
she was ready for sea, and at once entered upon
my duties without signing articles, that binding
ceremony being left until the day before departure. My return to fo'csle life was harder than
even I had feared, for this ship was manned almost

entirely by foreigners. Out of the entire ship's company of twenty-four, only two—myself and a Welsh A.B.—were Britons; and as Christianity had not denationalised me, I felt very sore about this, while as for any reasonable society on board I had none. The fo'csle was a babel of strange tongues, and the foreign officers were at no pains to show their dislike of me as an intruder in a ship under my own flag. While she remained in harbour things were not so bad, as I could cut off my ship life sharply every night at supper time (six P.M.) and seek the congenial society of my friends ashore. But even that made the contrast all the more painful. I prayed every day and all day, for I had got into a habit of talking to God in an almost familiar manner while at work, for a way out of this ship, for some opening in a ship where I should have at least one kindred soul with whom I could talk about the only subjects I now cared for.

And, as it has so often happened since, I got my desire. Not, either, to repent afterwards that my prayers had been granted, as I have done many times, but to enjoy my life at sea as never before, so that the memory of that voyage is one of the sweetest in my whole life. It happened in this way. At one of the Sunday evening meet-

ings in the sail-loft a huge Norwegian, Rasmus
Rasmussen by name, was so overcome by the
power of the Gospel that he broke down and wept
as—well, as a man does weep who, in the midst
of the sternest and most sorrowful conditions, has
been suddenly compelled to thus ease his labouring heart. After he was comforted, I was brought
into contact with him, and we were immediately
the firmest of friends. Every night we went ashore
together, for our ships occupied adjacent berths at
the railway pier, and eagerly drank in the lessons
we were taught by whoever happened to be telling
out the grand ideas of the Gospel, for we had not
yet grown very critical, and it all sounded good ;
also, we loved the singing, and would, had we not
been gently reminded of the time, have remained
in the places we went to, bare and comfortless as
they were in other respects, until midnight. Oh,
but it was a golden time, that babyhood of the
soul, when everybody and everything was seen
through a tremulous tender haze of light, the
Light which, coming into the world, lighteth every
man who does not wilfully remain blind.

Rasmussen, whose cumbrous name his shipmates had shortened to Jem, as the time drew
near for our parting grew very despondent. He

felt the same need as I did, and prayed continuously that a way might be found for me to come in his ship. Strangely, it never occurred to him to pray that he might come in mine. At last, only three days before I was to have signed articles in the 'Orpheus,' he came rushing on board in the dinner hour, radiant. Breathlessly he informed me that one of their fellows had been granted his discharge on account of illness; that he, Jem, had spoken to his skipper about me, and that I was to come on board at once and see that gentleman. I did so, and in five minutes I had agreed to sign in the 'West York' at ten shillings per month less than I was to have received in the 'Orpheus,' a reduction in wages which gave me no concern whatever. Yet this, to my mind, direct interposition of the Lord in my affairs in answer to my heart's desire, brought me the first unhappiness I had yet felt in regard to the behaviour of those whom I had learned to look upon as children of the living God.

It arose in this manner. Jem and I could hardly contain our joy until knock-off time, and immediately we were free we rushed off, changed our clothes, and ran to Aleck Falconer, the dear little barber, to tell him. He was as pleased as we

were, being one of those saintly souls who find their
highest delight in the joys of others. He gave
us a good meal, and when we had finished all three
went to the meeting together. Full of my news I
made haste to tell the assembled friends. But one of
them turned my heart to ice by saying censoriously,
' I don't think it was at all honourable of you to
break your word to the captain of the " Orpheus." '
I tried to explain that I had given two weeks' labour
for nothing, that I had made no agreement, that
other hands were easily obtained, and so on ; but
that unjust remark was not recalled, and my
sensitiveness made me feel that all my friends
were influenced by it in my disfavour.

This incident may, I fear, be regarded as trivial,
but all my conscious life I have had a passionate
hatred of injustice in any form. This particular
injustice, however, was worse to me than any other,
because it proceeded from one whom I had placed
upon an exalted pinnacle of holiness, and whose
good opinion I craved hungrily. And I did not
feel comforted by the knowledge that this unfavourable construction upon my action was utterly
undeserved. How deeply I felt it may be gauged
from the fact of my remembering it so clearly after
all these years.

However, the soreness soon wore off a bit, as no more was said on that subject, and we were presently the centre of a little knot of people interested in us, who were praying for our preservation from all evil on the passage home. It was good to hear Jem pray, the rugged Norse sentences pealing forth from his broad chest, while his great frame shook with emotion. Never in all my life have I seen a man so full of the overwhelming love of God. Up to within three weeks of this time he had been one of the most truculent blackguards that ever made trouble on board ship since he had first abandoned his fishing life for the deep water. He was to all appearance a lineal descendant of the old Norse Vikings—fierce, pitiless, without fear, and with a savage hatred of all restraint. His great size and strength, allied to his native ferocity, made him feared as well as hated; and even the awful experience of the Western Ocean packets had failed to tame him in the least. His body was covered with a network of scars, and his hands were gnarled and knotted like tree-roots. But the Master had spoken to him, choosing for the delivery of the message the alien tongue of an Englishman, whereof he only understood the simplest, commonest expressions, and now he was become as a little child who has been reared in an atmosphere of love. I have often heard of 'miracles of grace,' and I have seen many men to whom such a description might be applied justly, but Rasmus Rasmussen, of Bergen, common sailor, towered above them all as does a full-rigged ship over a ten-ton yacht.

He was so happy in the thought that I was coming with him that I did not dare to explain how much I had been hurt by the wrong construction put upon my action, and his loving interest in all that I did gave me most exquisite pleasure. So that, after all, I spent a happy evening, returning to the 'Orpheus' full of gratitude in the thought that it was for the last time. The next day was Sunday, and rising at four A.M. I dressed and went ashore, climbing up to the top of Flagstaff Hill, at the apex of the peninsula which separated the little cove of Port Chalmers from the estuary that leads up to the city of Dunedin. And there, alone in the sweet freshness of the morning, I remained for two hours, saturated with an unspeakable joy. The beauty of land and sea and sky as the rising of the sun touched it with celestial gold, the waking of the birds, and, above all, the intimate certain sense of the presence of God in His, to me, recently-discovered capacity of loving, tender Father, settled down upon my soul and filled me with such happiness as I think must be a foretaste of heaven. Unexplainable, indefinite, but a recompense for any amount of hardship, this living the new life communicated by the touch of Jesus. Human language, even at its highest and best, is totally inadequate to express this inexpressible joy, but I believe that all those who have claimed their blood-bought right of brotherhood to the Son have, according to their capacity, experienced it. If they have not, I should be inclined to doubt their full appreciation of the value of that world-sacrifice, that supreme altitude of love shown to all men by Jesus Christ.

That afternoon, at Jem's earnest solicitation, I went on board my new ship to supper. I found beside Jem that there were four Scotchmen—one working his passage home—a middle-aged gentleman, who had blasted his own career with drink at home, and had been working back through suffering to penitence in this far country. Of the other three, two were young men of about my own age, full of spirits and manly vigour; and one was a heavy, good-tempered fellow of small capacity. There were besides a stout, masterful German, a loutish hobbledehoy, who called himself a Cockney, and a cheery little pagan from that land of piety,

Cornwall. All these new acquaintances looked at me with great curiosity. They had heard, of course, that I was a Holy Joe of the most poisonous brand, and that, combined with their newly-born wonder at the radical change in Jem's behaviour, was quite enough to make them regard the coming passage with extraordinary interest.

For my own part, while I was rather nervous about my reception, I felt deeply grateful that my course was thus made plain. My colours were not only displayed, but nailed to the mast. If I proved recreant to them, I should not only be self-condemned, but I should be utterly despised by even the most godless among my shipmates ; for I have often seen it proved that while men may jeer at a Christian and try their utmost to make him fall, they honour him most highly if he stands firm. If he does fall, his lot is most unhappy. He feels that he is not only a traitor to the principle he has openly professed, that he is a living testimony to the inefficiency of the Gospel to save men from sin in the eyes of those who are its enemies, but he has lost his soul-satisfying joy, and in its stead he has the misery of knowing himself an enemy of his best Friend, while unable to gain the friendship of his worst Enemy. If a man goes

on board a ship where no one knows anything
of him, and is immediately plunged into the usual
welter of dirty and blasphemous talk, he is greatly
tempted to keep his Christianity to himself from the
cowardly dread of persecution. Where, however,
as in the present instance, his profession is known
beforehand, that danger is mercifully spared him.

So I bade my shipmates a cheery good evening,
which they returned in rather doubtful tones.
Then I bowed my head over my plate, and silently
thanked God for my food. Afterwards I joined
in the conversation, and did my best to be agree-
able and amusing, succeeding in removing the
impression that a Christian must of necessity be a
dour kill-joy, to whom a hearty laugh was a
grievous sin. A most enjoyable supper - hour
passed, during which I monopolised most of the
talk with various yarns of my adventures, especially my farming. But at the close of the meal,
strangely enough, I felt depressed and unhappy.
The fear that I had in some way dishonoured my
Master by a multitude of words wherein no mention
was made of His goodness to me, came upon me
as a dark cloud comes over the sun, and I put up
an earnest prayer that the Master would set a
watch over my lips and keep me from offending

with my tongue.   Doubtless there was something
morbid and self-worrying about this, but experience has proved that the desire to please by an
ability to talk well is often a trap to catch the
unwary young Christian.   Or ever he is aware he
is trembling upon the verge of some undesirable,
inconvenient (in the Gospel sense) misuse of
speech, and his carelessness is certain to be noted
by someone who will use it against him presently.

However, in the sweet sorrow of that evening's
meeting, knowing it to be the last, in parting with
so many dear friends, my temporary disquiet was
speedily forgotten, and I returned on board with
Jem, full of an abiding joy, all the more real because it was so quiet.   It was nearly midnight before
Jem and I turned in, for we sat on the fo'csle-head in
the moonlight and prayed turn-about, or, rather,
I should say, we held conversations with the Lord
in the fullest sense of His nearness to us, a sense
that was entirely independent of externals.

In the afternoon of the next day we sailed,
burdened with blessings, and wafted seawards by
a beautiful south-west wind.   We were bound for
Portland, Oregon, in ballast, expecting a passage
of about sixty days.   And so auspiciously commenced the most delightful voyage I ever made.

CHAPTER VII

HALCYON DAYS

THERE is one good rule that should never be neglected by any sea-farer upon joining a ship. It is to 'show willing.' A bad impression once made by a new-comer upon his shipmates takes a long time to remove, if it ever is; generally it clings throughout the voyage. But the need for proving at once that you are an acquisition to the ship's company is much more imperative in the case of a Holy Joe. Sailors, being in many respects exactly like people ashore, always expect that the Christian shall be perfect in every detail, not only of what they consider to be godliness, but also in ability, strength, and endurance. It is, after all, but a left-handed method of showing their appreciation of the worth of Christianity. They may jest and scoff at the idea of a man loving God and serving Him, not from fear of punishment, but from inbred affection and the working of the new life just communicated by the Spirit, but since they look for nothing less than perfection from a Christian, it needs no argument to prove that in some misty way they believe in its ability to make a man perfect.

Fortunately for me, I found myself in the same watch as Jem and the two smart young Scotchmen, Ballantyne and Turner. The two latter, though possessing not the slightest pretence to be considered godly, were most amiable fellows, as well as being hard-working, practical seamen. And when they found that not only could I do my duty with the best of them, but that I never hung back from a job, they showed their satisfaction in unmistakable fashion, and we were as comfortable together as four men could possibly be. Jem they teased unmercifully at times, but quite good-naturedly. That was only to be expected, as according to his own confession he had been just a rowdy ruffian on the passage out, and many of his doings still remained fresh in their minds. It was easy to see, however, that they were much puzzled at his sweetness of temper, his uniform cheerfulness and eagerness to do all that in him lay to justify his high profession. Nothing could shake his steadfast joy. We had rough weather almost immediately after leaving Port Chalmers, and, as usual, shipped a lot of water. One afternoon, just as we had finished dinner, Jem stepped out of the fo'csle (I call it a fo'csle, though it was a house in the middle of the main-deck, from sea-usage), and as he did so a big sea came hurtling over the side and drenched him to the skin. He made to run forward, and struck with all his force the bare toes on his right foot against a bolt of iron sticking up three inches out of the deck. All he said was, 'Tank God, tank God.' When he returned to the shelter of the fo'csle, Ballantyne said cheerfully, 'Fats gane wrang wi' ye, mahn? Are ye strucken doomb? Let's hae a few bit prayers fra ye. Ye haena forgotten hoo to say them, sewerly?'—meaning, I take it, some of the blasphemous expressions that would have rushed in a torrent from his mouth at such an accident on the passage out. But Jem's reply was as unexpected by his tormentor as it was disconcerting. For he dropped upon his knees immediately and cried, 'Dear Fader Gott, jou know I haf been zo bat, zo fery bat. I haf been blag lige pitch. I tink bat, speak bat, do bat all day, efery day. Unt den jou make me know jou lofe me, jou make me see mineselluf yoost as I vas, unt I been afrait. But now I know, glory to Gott, I know de blag sin is gone. I am all nice and vite inside, unt I don't afrait any more. Unt Billy ask me to pray liddle; tank you so much, dear Yesus, for dat. I vill be glat to break my feets efery day for dat, if I might get de shanse to pring him along to you. Dear Himmelsky Fader, bless him unt save him, and bless unt safe Bob, too, unt all my dear shipmates, unt all my dear broders and sesters in Port Chalmers, unt may ve all come togedder in jou big house up dere soon, for Yesus Christ's sake. Amen.'

My hearty 'Amen' echoed his, but beside that there was no sound. Our two watchmates were profoundly impressed, and I fancied I could see a tear glittering in Ballantyne's eye. As for Jem, his face was shining and the tears were streaming down as if indeed the well-spring of living waters had risen so high that it was visibly overflowing. Not another word was spoken. We all turned in, and were soon asleep.

That night I had myself what I considered, rightly I think, another practical proof of my surety in the Lord. It was blowing stiffly, and we

K

were carrying a press of canvas to get north out of the bad weather. Shortly after four bells we hauled down the flying jib and I sprang out along the boom to furl it. I was sitting astride the boom facing aft, my back strained against the downhaul, when suddenly it gave way with me. The sail slipped through my fingers and I fell backwards, hanging head downwards over the seething tumult of shining foam under the ship's bows, suspended by one foot. But I felt only high exultation in my certainty of eternal life. Although death was only divided from me by a hair's-breadth, and I was acutely conscious of the fact, it gave me no sensation but joy. I suppose I could have hung there no longer than five seconds, but in that time I lived a whole age of delight. But my body asserted itself, and with a desperate gymnastic effort I regained the boom. How I furled the sail I don't know, but I sang at the utmost pitch of my voice praises to God that went pealing out over the dark waste of waters. When I got inboard again the second mate was waiting on the fo'csle. Jem and Ballantyne were aloft furling the main-topgallant sail, and he, hearing my song, had come forrard, thinking I wanted help. When I told him

I had only been singing, he looked curiously at me, as if he thought I must be mad, but he said nothing, going aft again and leaving me to my solitary look-out. No, not solitary, for in those days I was never lonely. My sweetest hours were spent with no visible person near. And at that hour especially I had been so near to the consummation of all my hopes that I had caught a glimpse of the beyond, and the revelation had fed me full of speechless happiness.

Meanwhile my position in the ship was very pleasant. The skipper was most gracious. An admirable seaman, as well as a sincere Christian, he won my heart at once, although as yet no word had passed between us except in the way of business. But when Sunday came and we were all gathered aft on the quarter-deck, the weather having bettered greatly, he seemed to be transfigured into some beloved patriarch. No wonder I loved him. For he was the first officer of a ship that I had ever been shipmate with who really tried to honour God by holding a meeting for worship with his men. He had dressed himself as for going ashore, and I could see his eye lighten with pleasure as he saw that we had all made

ourselves as spruce as we could.   His countenance
fell, however, when Cockney came shuffling aft
late.   He was dirty and unkempt as usual.

But as if he put resolutely away any feelings at
variance with the solemnity of the service he was
about to perform, he turned to his extemporised
desk and gave out a hymn.   Now by this time I
knew a large number of Sankey's little collection
as it was then, and so I had no difficulty in raising
the tune.   How we did sing, to be sure!   Sailors
are naturally fond of singing, and the choruses of
these spirited sacred songs especially appeal to
them, so that, although we were but a handful in
number, quite a surprising volume of sound went
up into the bright sky of that pleasant Sunday at
sea.   A shock awaited me, however, when the old
gentleman opened a big prayer-book and began to
read the morning service of the Church of England.
For I had heard that he was a Methodist, and I
did not then know that many Methodists use the
Church Service, believing with John Wesley that
they have every right to do so.   Still, I should not
have minded that had he been able to read, but,
alas! he read those beautiful words worse than
ever I have heard them read in church, and that is

saying a great deal. Worse than that, he had that peculiarly exasperating trick of reading words into the matter before him that did not exist there, a trick I have often observed in readers, but the reason for which is a mystery. Sometimes his interpolations made nonsense of the prayers, sometimes they made worse. But, in spite of all that, his evident sincerity, pathetic earnestness, and great reverence made everyone feel that the service was real, that God was being worshipped in spirit and in truth.

After the service was over the old man called upon Cockney, and inquired in no gentle tones what he meant by coming aft to service in that disgraceful rig. He replied feebly that he had no time to clean himself. Then the skipper's anger waxed hot. Because it was a miserable lie. In that ship we were allowed the whole of Saturday afternoon to wash and mend, to the end that no man should complain that he was obliged to steal time from his watch below or excuse himself for being dirty. And I saw at once why we were so comfortable. For the reason that being a Christian had not, as it so often does through a wrong conception of its aims, taken from the skipper his firm conviction that it was righteous to keep discipline and punish evil-doers. His language to the delinquent Cockney was scathing and personal in the last degree, and that wastrel fairly writhed under it, showing, at any rate, that he had not lost all sense of shame. And when he got forrard his shipmates' remarks were not calculated to soothe him. They all looked upon him as a disgrace to a good ship.

After all, Cockney's shortcomings did not concern us in the starboard watch. All four—that is, Jem, Ballantyne, Bob, and myself—had by this time got to know each other well, and with that knowledge came great mutual respect. We had arrived at that comfortable point when no one was afraid or ashamed to say that he didn't know how to do such and such a piece of work because of being jeered at. We had also the proud consolation of knowing that whatever was to be done with the ship in our watch we could do and would, at any physical cost to ourselves, rather than have all hands on deck. I don't know whether the second mate, who was the old man's son, appreciated as he ought to have done his smart young watch, but I am sure the skipper did. His beaming face when we shortened or set sail under his eyes was delightful to see. More than that, he had found that he might be fatherly and friendly towards us without the slightest danger of our taking a mean advantage of his good nature. And when a merchant skipper finds a crew like that he has found a treasure. Unhappily such crews are exceedingly rare. But then so are skippers such as he was. The second mate, on the other hand, could never resist the temptation to 'haze' or 'work up' my comrade Jem. Of course, this was not to be wondered at, seeing what a handful Jem had been on the outward passage, and taking into consideration the fact that the second mate had not a weakness for forgiving people who had offended him, as he would have said. Apparently it made no difference to Jem, whose new-born patience and loveable temper could by no means be disturbed, but it certainly gave me some hot twinges, as the sight of injustice has ever done.

All these trifles, however, melted away each evening, when Jem and I, creeping in under the shelter of the top-gallant fo'csle, held our intimate communion with Him whom we knew to be our Saviour-Brother. Our surroundings were as far

removed from the conventional idea of a place of
worship as could well be, for in this ship the
owner had refused to house his sailors in a place
only fit for pigs or non-perishable stores, and consequently the top-gallant fo'csle, or space beneath
the small raised deck over the bows of the ship,
was unoccupied. It was like a cave of the winds.
But we looked forward to our meeting there with
the Presence each evening with great joy, and
would often sit after prayer and an almost murmured song of praise, in perfect silence while slow
sweet tears of unutterable joy trickled down. I am
painfully aware that many will be unable to refrain
from smiling sarcastically at these words, many
more will utterly refuse to believe them, others will
want explanation and proof. But none of these
things can alter the facts as I have recorded them
one jot. We were young, ignorant, and unlettered ;
our theology might have been summarised in two
lines of book print. We made mistakes, we were
continually condemning ourselves for idle words,
for harboured thoughts of evil, and but that we
were mercifully out of the reach of temptation I
have no doubt we should have had an enormously
increased list of things to be repented of.

Yet, as far as a man may, I solemnly affirm that we were both as near perfect happiness as a man can be in this world. Reverently, as becomes one who feels that he is treading upon holy ground, I declare that at times in those solemn moments of silence the tide of happiness rose so high that we were fain to ask the Lord to stay His hand, the frail creature could hold no more and live. This sensation, feeling, emotion, what you will, you who can find a scientific explanation for most things, may have been easily referable to pre-existing causes. Of that I know nothing. I only know that it was not in the least artificial, that it came without any attempt of ours to produce it, that it filled our hearts, or our souls, whatever you will, with love, joy, and peace, and that it made us in every sense better men.

Another thing which I think deserves especial mention was the absence of all external human aids or incitements to religious fervour. Undoubtedly this opens up a tremendously controversial question, which, of course, I do not, cannot, pretend to discuss; but surely a religion that requires any external adjuncts, whether sacerdotal or not, cannot be what Christianity rightly claims to be, of universal application. The sailor, for instance, is almost always placed in a position where any external human aid to religion is out of the question. More than that, his surroundings are in most cases distinctly inimical to any outward religious observances whatever. Even the repetition of stated prayers at set times, the regular study of the Bible, is exceedingly difficult, often impossible. Here it is that the unique character of true Christianity manifests itself. It makes the struggling, sinful man or woman realise that a new element has entered into them, a new life which emanates direct from God, and is consequently directly and entirely hostile to evil. It warns the recipient of this highest blessing in the world that this free gift of an indwelling power unconquerable, not to be deteriorated in any way, does not convert him into a righteous automaton, such as some sceptics scoffingly inquire why God did not make in the beginning of things. It tells him that the motive power as well as the resisting force of this new life depends, as far as he is concerned, upon his encouragement of it or the reverse. It bids him beware of the fatal assumption that now he is, as it were, inoculated against the deadly virus of sin, or that all obligation to work out his own salvation is taken off his shoulders.

True, there are many mistakes made, mistakes of the most awful kind, for when did man ever fail to convert blessings into curses from sheer perversion? As, for instance, when one hears people calmly rise in meetings and proclaim with mountainous pride that for so many years they have lived without offending the Most Holy One in thought, or word, or deed. But these misunderstandings of plain words in no sense make the word of God void. Rather they point to the inherent tendency of humanity to refuse the good and choose the evil, or, worse still, deliberately pervert the good to evil uses.

Of course, the life led by Jem and myself could not fail to be noticed and commented upon by our two watchmates. But they never said a word to us. Only, I think, if we had been more observant, a little less selfishly content with our own happiness, we might have seen that something was going to happen. The ship had got into fine weather—into the south-east trade winds of the Pacific—and our night watches on deck were full of delight. There were an apprentice and a

boy in our watch, who both steered in fine weather,
an arrangement that made it often possible for the
whole four of us to sit on the fo'csle-head and
talk throughout the whole of our vigil. And we
did talk. We did not want to sleep. We sat
and discussed according to our ability the wonders
of all around us, and I finished up from my
memory all that would come of what I had read.
The usual topics of sailor talk were never so much
as mentioned between us, but I am sure neither
Ballantyne nor Bob felt the loss of that ; as for
Jem and myself, the taste for such things had
been taken away.

So the days rolled delightfully by until it came
to pass one night that I was sitting on the capstan
on the fo'csle head keeping my look-out, my gaze
fixed upon the dim blue vacancy ahead. I was
singing softly 'God loved the world of sinners
lost' and enjoying myself indescribably. The
vessel was only moving through the water about
four knots an hour, and from the absence of swell
she was so steady that her progress was almost
motionless. To port was the pure calm disc of
the full moon, her silver glow dulling the stars
near and spreading a glittering way right up to

the ship. All over the rest of the heavens the stars were shining in the clear sky, except just around the horizon's edge, where there was a border of fleecy clouds. It was a full-heart night.

Suddenly into my meditations came the sound of a broken voice, and turning sharply round I saw Ballantyne standing near. By the bright light of the moon I could see that his rugged face was working, all its jovial dimples gone, and down his cheeks big tears chased each other. Now one thing is always noticeable in the truly converted man or woman ; their hearts grow very soft, their pity great for anyone in distress. So I was deeply moved, and springing off my perch I clutched his hand, eagerly inquiring what was the matter. All he could say was that he was an awful sinner. He wanted to tell me what his life had been, but I would not hear. I told him that I had no right to be his confessor, and that his telling me could do no good. Maybe I was wrong, but that was how I felt about it. What I could do to comfort him I did, telling him exactly how I had found peace, and assuring him that he need not weary himself in trying to force an open door, that the Lord was far more anxious to receive him than he was to come, deeply stirred as I could see him to be. I was afraid to talk too much, however, because I had seen people actually confused out of all comprehension, and I had been taught by experience that at the supreme moment of the birth of a soul, the nurse must stand aside and allow the Physician to do His work unhindered. There will be plenty of scope for nursing afterwards. I believe we stood in perfect silence for about ten minutes while I was sending up an incessant stream of wordless petitions that it might please the Lord to set this anxious soul at liberty.

Presently he spoke: 'Tom, lad, let's hae a bit pray'r frae ye.' I gladly responded, but even as I knelt I could not help remembering the occasion so shortly before when he had put almost the same request to Jem in the hope of hearing that much-tried man give vent to his feelings in some of the foul words that had been his usual speech. But resolutely pushing away the hindering reflection, I said, 'Dear Father, here's poor Willie Ballantyne brought face to face with you at last. You've done it yourself, and no one but himself can prevent him from being set free. I needn't ask you to save him, you've done all that; but I

do ask you to make him see that it is so.   Loving
Lord, you've been pleading with him for a long
time.   Make him give up struggling against you,
make him as happy as you make everybody who
give themselves right up to you.   And we'll bless
you and praise you with all our hearts, with all
the new words and powers you've given us.
Amen.'

I had no sooner finished speaking than Ballantyne broke in : 'Lord Jesus Christ, I ken ye've
sauvit me.   I canna feel't, ma heid's all dizzy like,
but I'm believin' wut ye've said about nut ca'asting
oot ony puir vratch 'at comes t' ye.   A'am's bad's
ah can be, a drucken, swearin', feckless loun, there
isna onythin' tae be said fur ma 'at's guid.   But
ah ken fine 'at ye love me fur all ahm sae bad.
Here ah a'am, tak ma, an' make somethin' oot o'
ma, fur ah've made an awfu' mess o' mysel.   Amen.'
And springing to his feet he kissed me, while I
hardly knew whether I was in the body or out of
it.   All I knew and realised most profoundly was
that He who came to do the will of His Father
was doing it now, and no one else had any hand
in the wonderful work at all.

As soon as ever we had quieted down, if that

be the correct expression to use where all had been so quiet, I said, 'May I go and tell Jem, Willie?' 'Ay,' he answered readily, 'ye may that, Tom.' In a moment I sprang off the fo'csle and flew round the corner of the house, coming crash up against Jem's broad chest with a force that nearly knocked all the breath out of my body. What little remained was speedily dispersed, for Jem, flinging those long arms of his around me, gave me a hug like that of a grizzly bear, so that I hung limp and helpless across his body while he gasped, in broken tones, 'Bob's foun' de Lord. Bob's foun' de Lord.' Then my condition alarmed him, and he sat me gently down, full of solicitude as to whether he had hurt me. I thought my ribs were cracked, but, finding I was all right, I eagerly inquired how this strange thing had come about. He told me that for the last hour he had been pleading with Bob in consequence of a question the latter had put to him almost identical with that asked me by Ballantyne. And this was the result. Then I told him my wonderful news, and for a few moments I thought he would have a fit. In the midst of our mutual rejoicings our two chums joined us, and from thence till eight bells we had such a prayer-meeting as I have never attended before or since.

The bell brought it to a close, but when we were relieved and went below we could not sleep. We sat up in our bunks and sang as if we would burst our breasts, as the bird sang, of whom George Macdonald says:

> 'Glad is so glad that it turns to ache :
> Out with it, song, or my heart will break.'

Our shipmates of the other watch came in and looked sourly at us, the big German especially. How well I remember his sarcastic question, 'Vell, jou all goes mat, ain'd id?' When we tried to tell them what had happened they went out, firmly convinced that we had gone mad, and muttering disgustedly. But what did we care? What did anything matter now? The Lord had lifted up the Light of His countenance upon us, and our cups were overflowing. It was the tongue of the dumb singing. But to try and explain it would be as easy as making a colour-blind man appreciate the glories of a tropical sunset.

L

CHAPTER VIII

TESTING TIME COMES

AFTER what has already been said it will be readily imagined that our watch below thenceforward was a happy time. There were no more meetings in the dark shade of the topgallant fo'csle for Jem and me. There was no need, because we were all of one mind. And now I was able to make good use of my one talent, that of reading fairly well. There was a ship's library on board, but like so many of the libraries placed on board ship in the old days, it was mostly stuffed with rubbish, goody-goody stuff that even a healthy child would 'scunner' at. So we were thrown back upon the Bible, and a very good job too. For there is no book that contains so much good reading as this, even when a man reads without the eyes of his understanding being opened. And when he drinks it in as we did no words can tell of his appreciation. Having found out that searching the Scriptures is no mere perfunctory task, the performance of which at stated intervals puts a certain amount of righteousness to his credit, but an ever-growing delight, the education of the young Christian may be said to be fairly under way.

One book, however, I must exempt from the sweeping condemnation passed upon our stock. It was a child's book, truly, but its effect upon us was marvellous. Every word went right home to our hearts, all soft as they were, and I am sure if Miss Hesba Stretton had seen four rough young sailors choking red-eyed over the story she has woven round ' Jessica's First Prayer,' she would have also been compelled to allow her eyes to overflow with sympathetic joy.

For some time the other watch refused to associate with us. They could not help noticing that we were smarter and more energetic than ever at our work, they were obliged to admit that we were more obliging and courteous as a watch than we had been, and that we never kept them waiting at eight bells for relief, but for nearly a month they held aloof. But they tired of that and gradually came round uneasily, because we always stopped any questionable yarns. At last, finding that our sanity could not be denied, and that our sudden bursting forth into song was not merely a flash in the pan but an abiding alteration, they reverted to their old companionship, only clearing out precipitately if one of us ventured upon any remarks of a religious nature. We did not tell the 'old man,' but, bless him, he soon found it out and it made him so happy that his face seemed to wear a perennial smile.

We had rather a long passage to Portland as passages of sailing ships go—sixty-four days—but none of the starboard watch, I am sure, ever spent a tedious hour. For my part, in addition to the usual duties of a foremast hand when he is below of making and mending his clothes, washing them and taking his turn as cook of the mess, I was endeavouring to teach myself navigation, with an occasional hint from the mate, an amiable little Jerseyman. So that, take it all round, I was kept fairly busy, and my watch also found plenteous employment in one way and another. We got less sleep than usual, but our waking hours were lived, not flung away. As to the 'intolerable tedium of a long voyage,' no sailor worth his salt ever uses such words. There should never be any tedium at sea.

At last, with the usual amount of excitement, as none of us had been there before, we made the bar of the Columbia River, and far inland saw the snowy peak of Mount St. Helena towering purely skyward like a conical stationary cloud, being only about ninety miles away. We took steam and towed in across the bar, learning with a good deal of satisfaction that we were shortly to proceed up the noble river before us to the city of Portland. Satisfaction for two reasons : we wanted to see the river scenery, and we did not fancy the loneliness of Astoria, the port at the river's mouth, where one large ship, the 'Desdemona,' was lying loading. It may seem strange that a sailor should talk about the loneliness of a harbour after the vast solitudes of the ocean, but it is so. The privacy of the sea he takes for granted—it must be so ; but an unpeopled harbour he resents—it is as if he were being defrauded of his right to company after being so long away from any other than that of his shipmates.

For myself, I longed more than anything else to view the scenery of this wonderful part of the world. It was new to me, and I was told that it was very beautiful. And ever since the awakening of my soul I had grown more and more in love with the beautiful things of earth, and sea, and sky. What people call the æsthetic sense of beauty in its true light is, I believe, more strongly fostered by the knowledge of the love of God than anything else. I know of people whose religion is of that gloomy, distorted, God-dishonouring kind that almost looks upon enthusiastic admiration for the work of God in creation as sin. Poor souls, they mean well, but what envious spirit can have bewitched them into the appalling belief that He who considered the lilies and the sunset glow, spread the world with beauty indescribable, enriching every nook of earth with loveliness for His own delight, should desire His dear children to blind themselves for His pleasure! No, I do not believe that there is any education in a love of the beautiful so thorough, so effective, as that gained by an acquaintance with Jesus Christ.

In due time we left our moorings, and in tow of one of the stately, towering river-steamers that Americans delight in, we departed. The 'Willamette Chief' our imposing motor—it seemed almost irreverent to speak of her as a tug, so splendid did she appear by our side—glided up stream against the considerable current with great ease, at no time exerting all her power. That great stern-wheel of hers seemed irresistible.

The view as we turned bend after bend was truly enchanting, especially to me, whose opportunities of looking upon inland scenery had been so small. Those solemn, endless avenues of pines coming right down to the water's edge and reflecting the tall pillars of their stems in the placid surface of the river, especially appealed to me—I could not help comparing them with the vastly different vegetation on the banks of the Clarence, in New South Wales, up which I so often steamed when lamp-trimmer in the 'Helen McGregor.' I do not remember how long we were towing up : I only know that the time seemed very short, and before we could realise that the long upward tow was nearly at an end, Portland, with its rows of double-tiered wharves, its fine buildings and clusters of shipping, burst into view. But who is this coming off in a four-oared boat, bumping alongside, and climbing over the rail with a strange air of proprietorship ? Without taking any notice of the after-guard, he strolls forrard and introduces himself to us as we all stand grouped together staring at the city. He is, it appears, one James Turk, who keeps a respectable boarding-house for seamen, to which he has come to invite us. He informs us casually that wages for A.B.'s are at present forty dollars a month, and that the paltry formality of getting a legal discharge need not trouble us. It appears they don't go much on discharges here. 'An' ye'll git tew mont's' advance, y'know, 'fore ever ye go aboard,' he adds.

This last is rather much for me to listen to silently, so I say, with the utmost politeness; 'Who'll get two months' advance, did you say?'

'Annybody as ships here,' he replied excitedly; 'you ef ye like ter be man enough t' git yer dunnage an' stip into my boat thet's 'long side.'

'Thanks,' I murmured, 'I thought the boarding master usually got the advance, and the sailor that was fool enough to have anything to do with him got a broken head and a few bruises if he ventured to ask for what belonged to him.' Swift as thought the wild-beast stood revealed—man-stealer, murderer, criminal of loathliest shape. Can any term of opprobrium be too severe to apply to these demons of the American ports, whose awful trade has been a blot upon the fair fame of the great Republic for so many years. This particular devil burst forth into a flood of flaming blasphemies against us all, and myself in particular, lurid language to which none of us answered a word. Until presently big Jem stepped forward quietly and said: 'My vrient, jou vants de crace of Gott fery batt.'

Shall I ever again see such a transformation? The truculent villain looked stupidly first at Jem, then at us all, one after the other, and then wearily turned away, ejaculating his formula: 'Well, God damn my soul t' hell.' So he passed from our ken and we saw him no more. But afterwards we heard that this particular specimen of the Pacific Coast boarding master had a reputation for evil-doing second to none in all that foul fraternity. And we were assured that we might be exceedingly grateful that none of us had been waylaid by his orders and brutally done to death. But I do not know. It has been my experience that in most cases where sailors have been thus evilly treated it has been because they themselves have been consenting parties in a measure, that they have willingly gone to those places where they were most easily trapped. Poor brother seamen ! as if you had not sufficient enemies without you yourselves giving those enemies all the facilities they require to work you harm.

For two days we did not feel inclined to go ashore. There was much to be done, and when the day's work was over it was pleasanter to sit upon the fo'csle head and smoke than to go rambling we knew not whither. But on the third day Bob and I were painting the ship's bottom, or as much of it as we could get at, with some vile patent compound that could not be thinned like ordinary paint. It was so thick and ropy that no brush could spread it, and we were fain to plaster it on the iron plates with our bare hands. To do this we stood upon a raft which was fastened so that it lay between our bows and the wharf. We must have presented a gruesome sight with that filthy green compound besmearing our arms and our clothing. But we were in our usual good-humoured state of mind, and as we plastered the paint on we sang cheerily, heartily, for we were out of hearing of the deck, and there was no in-fraction of discipline in our so doing. Presently we became aware that someone was joining in the chorus of one of our songs—'The home over there,' I think—and looking up we saw a well-dressed young man, who was sitting on the edge of the wharf, dangling his legs. As soon as we saw him he stopped and entered into conversation by saying, 'I can't think what has come over you British sailors ; you seem so different to the men who man our vessels.' I replied that I was afraid there was not much to choose between us, but he cut me short by saying, 'Oh, yes, there is. For some time past I have been noticing the behaviours of the ships' crews that come here, and I have always found a better class of men in the British vessels. But that is not solely the reason why I spoke to you. I am a Christian, and, although I am a landsman, earning my living in a book-store, I have also a great affection for sailors. Now we have no special organisation here for the religious benefit of seafaring men, I am sorry to say, so that I devote what leisure I have to strolling about the wharves, and whenever I find a sailor religiously inclined I invite him up to our meeting, which is quite unsectarian and evangelical in character. Will you come?'

Bob looked at me inquiringly, and I, feeling that this was a heaven-sent opportunity, said that I thought I could answer for three of my ship-mates coming. For myself, I would be delighted. Then our new-found friend promised to call for us at seven that evening, bade us 'Good-bye, and God bless you,' and departed. Jem and Ballantyne were quite excited at the prospect when Bob and I informed them, and punctually to the moment we all stepped ashore, although it had been a terrible job getting that loathsome paint off. Our friend turned up in good time, and away we went over the most curious road I had ever trod. It seemed to be composed of planks laid on mud, which, being fairly fluid, had an unpleasant knack of spurting up at one through the interstices be-tween the planks. And as the place was none too well lighted, this happened far too frequently. We cared little for the badness of the way, being much too intently occupied with anticipations of our visit, and although the way was long also our eager conversation prevented us from noticing that either.

When we arrived at the building, which was quite palatial after our bare sail-loft at Port

Chalmers, we found that our fame had preceded us. The warmth of our welcome from about two hundred people present quite overcame us, and for the moment we felt almost sorry we had come, we were so shy and awkward. We speedily found that, as at Port Chalmers, there were representatives of all the religious denominations in the place except the Roman Catholic, but these Yankees were far more demonstrative. They did not believe in hiding their religious fervour under a cloak of conventional decorum. They behaved as if they thoroughly enjoyed themselves, and although nothing was said or done to which any real Christian could sensibly object, I must confess I found myself considerably astonished. The quaint sayings of some of the speakers almost made me choke with suppressed laughter, until a grave-looking speaker who had just made some, to me, screamingly funny remark, saw my suffering and said : 'Young friend, laef just 's much 's y' want to. God don't begrudge any of His children a laef; don't you believe He does for one moment. 'N He don't want the old devil t' have a monopoly of so healthful a thing as laefter is. Rejoice in the Lord always, an' again I say rejoice, wa'nt said t' induce people t' go round lookin' 's if they'd jest planted a number of their folks, an' the balance wuz mighty sick.'

So I laughed, shamefacedly at first, but heartily afterwards, as heartily as I and those that were with me joined in the singing and the praying. But presently we were filled with horror at a direct invitation to get up on the platform and tell the friends present something about our religious life at sea. I'm sure I do not know how I got upon the platform and found myself facing those eager upturned faces. My heart thumped against my ribs, and my mouth and tongue went dry and leathery. When at last I found my voice I hardly knew it, so hollow and strange it sounded. But the kindness of my audience was unbounded. One would have thought that they were listening to one of the finest efforts of their own splendid orators (and there seems to be something in the American climate that favours the development of oratorical gifts) by the way they behaved.

I really don't know what I did say. I tried to put my experience into words, and I know I did not take any of the foregoing speakers as a model. But that is all I can say. Then came a captain in the American Army—a noble fellow, thrillingly earnest, but with a tremendously rapid utterance and a most involved style. His speech made me wonder at myself for being so thick-headed as not to understand a word of it. But one of his similes I have never forgotten. I do not remember what it was intended to illustrate, but I fancy I can hear him now saying : ' It's like the man who told his boy he'd give him ten cents to learn the ten commandments, and a brick house with a marble front if he could understand 'em.' Many other quaint things he said, but suddenly he sat down, and while yet my mind was a-whirl with the wondrous incoherency of his discourse, he had been replaced by my brother Jem. Ah, that was a change indeed. For Jem only said in the simplest way that which the Lord gave him to say, and the fact that he spoke in an alien tongue, necessitating a double process simultaneously in his brain, did not hinder his discourse being of the most heart-searching kind.

As well as my memory serves me, he spoke as follows : ' Dear vrients. Jou haf ask me to tell jou vat de Lort haf done for me. How can I dis do ? Ven I tink of His gootness unt lofe, I haf

not vorts efen in mine own langvidge to speak of
it ; how den I can tell jou in Engelsch, vich I only
talk like any oder sailor-man.   But yet I not can
say no.   I vas a teufel, I dink vorse, because de
teufels dey haf no hope, unt I haf shut my soul up
from hope myselluf.   If dere is anyting bad I can
do I haf do it.   I haf hate de dear Fader Gott, I
haf hate all His beobles.   Oh, is dere any ting
bad I haf not do?   I vill say not any more apoudt
my sin, pecause I haf much shame for dem, and yet
I feel dat if I talk 'bout dem I vill tink mooch
of myselluf pecause I *haf* been so bad.   Unt
more, I vas so misbul.   I nefer haf no peace, I
nefer haf no res', I nefer haf no pleasure 'cept I
ked tronk unt fight, unt dat cos' all de money I
vork so hardt for.   Den I come to Port Chalmers
unt I go into de meetin', unt I hear a man say
dat de Lordt Jesus Christ is come to tell man vat
Gott is.   Dat Gott ton'd hate me, a'net vant me
to die unt go to hell, dat hell ain'd vatin' for me,
but Gott vaits allvus, unt dat He ben sorry dat I
vas not habby.   He tell me dat dere is only von
man can send me to hell unt dat is me myselluf,
unt dat if I come unt ket into His hants dere
ain'd no von, no not efen de Sattan himselluf, dat
can pull me 'vay 'gen.

'Unt vile I lissen unt hear effery vort, peliefing id's all true, 'pout somepody ellas, I hear a vort in here [striking his breast] dellin' me, "Jes, Yem, jou ben de man all dis for." Und I ton't vait anoder minit. I pelief id. I say, "Jes, Lord Yesus, I bin de man you die for. Unt now I bin coin' to gif myselluf all oop for you." Unt if any man say to me any more, "How jou know all dis?" I say to him, "How I know? Vat you tink id is keep me frum svearin', frum bein' bucko', from keddin' tronk, frum hatin' myselluf unt eferypody ellas? Jou ton't know? Vell, I do. Id bin de Lort Gott Allmighty. Nopotty ellas can do it. Unt now I vas yoost like a leedle shild. I haf lose de taste for de bad unt find id for de goot, tank Gott. Unt if I, dot vas so bad, unt tondt know anyting 't all, ked holt of dis goot ting who in de vorlt coin' to be left oud. Gott bless eferypotty, for Yesus Christ sake. Amen."'

The broken, halting words ceased, but their effect upon the audience was marvellously manifested. Talk about the efforts of oratory, the power to sway with magic words allied to the music of the human voice multitudes of people as the wind sways the corn. Wonderful the

M

gift, but here was a man hardly able to speak the language of his hearers, ignorant of all elocutionary rules, of any tricks of rhetoric, who had so gripped the hearts of his audience that they wept, almost writhed, under the fierce stress of their emotions. And as he descended from the platform the meeting broke up, for all present wanted to press his hand. And I, who dreaded intensely all forms of spasmodic emotional religion, mere play of feeling influenced by externals and evanescent as the ripple upon water when the wind dies away, was so profoundly moved that I was glad to get away into a corner and simmer down. Then the evening was wound up with the singing of the Doxology, and the four of us returned on board as if we were treading on air.

Henceforward, during our stay in Portland we went ashore every night and became most intimate with earnest Christian people of every sort. In fact, the time passed all too quickly. But of all the people that we met I think those who impressed us the most were of the class that laboured mightily with their hands. In all sorts of queer rooms we foregathered and held our prayer-meetings, praise-meetings, experience-meetings.

Never once were we allowed to feel that life was uninteresting. Never once did the idea occur to us, ' These people have had enough of our society, and we had better return to our ship and stay there.' All this happiness culminated on the day of our departure in the visit of every one of those acquainted with us who could get away for the purpose, assembling on the wharf to see us off. The old man, who had only a dim idea of how we had been employing our time, was astounded at the warmth of our farewells. We were all greatly touched, and those who know the reputation that Portland, Oregon, holds as regards the behaviour of seamen will agree with me that such a send-off must have caused quite a sensation.

So, again laden with blessings, we departed for home, for the long, long stretch down to the Horn and up again to the well-beloved group of islands in 51 N. We were exceptionally favoured by fine weather, having an almost ideal passage except as regards length. That we were much longer than usual was due solely to the fact that we had a patent machine on board for scrubbing the vessel's bottom while at sea. All sailors know how much the marine growth upon that part of the vessel

M 2

below the water hinders the progress of the ship. This machine was intended to do away with such hindrance. But, unhappily, it scraped off the anti-fouling composition as well as the weeds, barnacles, &c., with the result that on the bare iron the impediments accumulated at an astonishing rate. I have often wondered how it is that the marine growths prefer bare iron to anything else except bare wood for growing on. Ships that are sheathed with copper or yellow metal never get such masses upon them as do iron ships in at least half the time.

However, we reached Falmouth at last, all in excellent health and spirits, and were soon thronged with visitors from the captain's home, St. Ives. And this gave me, at any rate, a severe shock incidentally. For these visitors were all keenly religious, yet from the time they came on board until they left they talked scandal—wicked, withering scandal—of those they had left at home. And as we were working about amongst them we could not help hearing their conversation in full detail. The amount of harm it did among us I cannot estimate, but I feel sure that if those careless talkers had known how their slanderous tongues were influencing their hearers they would have repented bitterly. Years after I read a wonderful little book by an author whose name I have forgotten, entitled 'Death in the Pot.' It dealt with the terrible habit of scandal-mongering among some body of Dissenters to which the author belonged, and with great clarity of language pointed out the evil that was being done in this way. From my brief experience of that visit in the 'West York' I could heartily endorse every word of it.

But there was a powerful antidote at hand in the knowledge of those with whom I had lived and worked so long, who never said an unkind word of each other, or allowed backbiting in their hearing without standing up manfully for the maligned and absent one. The pity of this accursed habit is that it grows upon the hearer unless he fights tremendously against it. He begins to suspect that those whom he has so long trusted and loved are talking about him in his absence in the same way, and that he can repose confidence in no one. Enough, however, for the present on this unhappy theme. It was the only time in all my sea experience that I came across it, and the culprits were not sailors.

Orders came for us to proceed to Belfast, and with beautiful weather we proceeded to this, our final port. When we came up before the shipping master to be paid off, the old gentleman declared that in all his forty years' experience he had never seen so respectable and fit-looking a crew come to the pay table. At which our good old skipper was hugely delighted. But then came in that abominable break in our relations which is characteristic of the Merchant Service. Having learned to like each other, having proved our worth to the ship, we were now scattered to the four winds of heaven, because the ship did not want us until she was ready to go to sea again. And of course we none of us could take the risk of waiting in Belfast for her.

It was a sad parting. Ballantyne and Turner went home to their people in Scotland, and it was only three weeks ago that I saw Turner again after a lapse of twenty-four years. He is master of a splendid steamer, and has been so for several years. And through meeting him I heard from Ballantyne yesterday, whom I had also lost sight or sound of for the same period. Of Jem I must say a few parting words, but reserve them for the next chapter.

CHAPTER IX

HALTING ON THE UPWARD WAY

SAILORS get so accustomed to the pain of parting with their dear ones for long periods that they naturally become somewhat hardened, but for my own part I had never had anyone so dear to me as to make the pain of parting with them severe. It is true that I had in some measure given my affections to places instead of people, feeling always more or less sad at leaving a port that I had become accustomed to. But the breaking up of the 'West York's' crew made me feel more miserable than any such separation had hitherto done. I dreaded to lose Jem, yet I knew that it was inevitable. He had not been to his native place in Norway for many years, and was now firmly resolved to visit it and spread in his own language among his own countrymen the glorious news of what the Gospel of Jesus Christ had done for him. And here I must interpolate that only a few months ago I received a letter from Port Chalmers, written by Aleck Falconer, the whilom tender-hearted little barber, but now seamen's missionary in Dunedin, in the course of which he informed me that Jem had devoted his life to the spread of the Gospel in Bergen and had been an enormous power for good.

When the day of parting came, Turner and Ballantyne bade me an affectionate farewell, but restrained their feelings, after our island manner. None the less, I know that they both felt the breaking up of our happy family as deeply as I did. But when at last the hour for Jem's departure drew near he came silently up to me, and, taking my hand, drew me into his room.   Then without one word being spoken we fell on our knees and remained for some moments in unspoken prayer. At last, with a great sob, Jem burst out: 'Oh, dear Himmelsky Fader Gott, dou sees dat me an' mein dear broder here haf got to say goot-bye. Tondt let us efer forget von anoder.   Keep oos straight.   Keep oos full of dy lof.   Make oos boat strong as lions 'gainst de teufel an' lofing as dou art tovards all de people ve gomes alonkside of. Hellup oos to bear dis partin'.   Lort, dou knows id's fery hardt, after vat ve ben to each oder, but dy vill be allvus done. Dake dis mein broder into dy arms unt holdt, him dere tighdt. Tondt let him lost de schmile of dy face, no not for von minnit of his life. Unt den, dough ve nefer see von anoder in dis vorld any more, ve know ve meet again ven you vill be dere to keep oos and bless us vit dy bresence allvus. Lord Yesus bless him, bless me, bless all our shibmates and de dear vons ve leaf in Noo Seelant, unt pring oos all home togedder ven our vork ben done down here. Amen.'

Then he rose, caught me in his arms, pressed his streaming face to mine, and departed. I dropped into a chair and sat like one stunned. It was such a terrible wrench. It was my first great bereavement. And though we Britons pride ourselves on concealing our feelings, and cultivate a sort of pitying scorn of those who do not or cannot, there is something in the knowledge of the brotherhood of Christ that elevates friendship, sacred and lovely as that always is, into a purer, higher, holier atmosphere, making us understand the sublime lament of David for Jonathan. And by such means we obtain as in no other way a deeper insight into the meaning of the love of God for man. Deep in my heart I cherish the memory of several men whom I have loved, and who have loved me, because the love of the Father had drawn us together, and when I recall our perfect communion of heart I feel grateful to God for having allowed me to live that I might know how dear He can make His people one to another, how perfect is the happiness that such lofty love provides.

It was with a lonely heart that I also prepared to leave Belfast. Insensibly I had grown very dependent upon the love and sympathy of my three watchmates, and now that they were all gone the empty place refused to be filled. I could not at once fall back upon the never-failing companionship of Him who had promised that I should never seek in vain for true companionship any more. Being very human and weak, the longing for the love and sympathy of my fellows was great, and, lacking it, I was nearly miserable. Some strange impulse drew me London-wards. But I thought I would see Liverpool again on my journey thither—I suppose because I was curious to know how I should feel walking those stony-hearted streets no longer as a penniless outcast, but warmly clad and with twenty-five bright sovereigns in my pocket. So I took a deck passage in the 'Voltaic' for Liverpool, and enjoyed much the novel sensation of being a passenger, until, the night growing very cold, I climbed on to the 'fidley,' or grating over the stokehold, and tried to go to sleep. Very soon I was joined by an elderly pig merchant who was coming over with about a hundred of those useful but noisy beasts. No sooner had he got comfortably seated than he began mumbling an appalling litany of cursings and blasphemies, with no apparent object. For a little while I could hardly believe my ears, but being quickly assured of the horror of his language I remonstrated with him. The only result was to make him louder, and if possible more blasphemous than before. And then, to my own astonishment, I suddenly became furious. I felt such a savage outburst of anger as I had never known before in my life. I snatched at him and dragged him off the fidley, assuring him earnestly that if he didn't close his filthy mouth I would drop him down the stokehold. And he, taken by surprise, I suppose, obeyed, nor, as far as I am aware, did he speak another word all night.

On that gridiron-like couch we dozed uneasily, until just as morning dawned I awoke with a horrible choking sensation in my throat. I was covered with a thick layer of black ash that had risen from the stokehold when they damped down after cleaning fires, and my nostrils, ears and eyes seemed full of fine grit, and as there was no accommodation on board for deck passengers to wash I landed in Liverpool in this deplorable condition. Yet the experience did me good, for I now felt the satisfaction of being able to go and get renovated, be treated with the utmost courtesy, and emerge into the street again an independent, self-respecting man, because I had my hard earnings in my pocket and knew how to spend them.

I only stayed in Liverpool long enough to visit the scenes of my sufferings, and next day took train for London. Now, when my railway journeys about the country run into several thousands of miles each year, I often think regretfully of the abounding delight felt at that swift passage through the beautiful country, just clothing itself in all the beauty of spring. By the time that the train reached Willesden my eyes ached and burned with the intensity of my gaze over hill and dale, coppice, meadow and stream, yet I could have wished the journey had been three times as long. I went on to Liverpool Street from Willesden, left my dunnage there, and strolled out into the whirl of the great city, feeling utterly strange and forlorn. After aimlessly wandering about for some time, I found myself on London Bridge, in the company of that little line of vacant-looking people who may always be found gazing down upon the discharging steamers or the gliding barges. I stood among them looking vacant too, and feeling indeed like a stranger in a strange land. And it was not until I was thoroughly chilled and weary that I made up my mind to go West and seek a lodging. I found a decent furnished room in the neighbourhood of King's Cross, and there I remained for about three weeks, one of twenty single men who occupied rooms in the same house, going out early in the morning and returning to sleep—never becoming acquainted with each other, their very occupations enveloped in mystery, the only thing demanded of them by the hard-working, hard-featured landlady being that they should pay their rent punctually, come in quietly, and bring no doubtful visitors with them.

But it was a very lonely life. My circle of occupations was circumscribed greatly by my firm belief that theatres and music-halls were places of evil into which I dared not go, that public-houses were if anything worse, and that I had not one single acquaintance of either sex. So I read a good deal, went to all the museums, parks, gardens and such-like mildly exciting places of recreation, only visiting the docks one day to get my discharge in for another voyage. I left it with the chief officer of the 'Dartmouth,' a fine comfortable-looking old barque of about 900 tons register, bound for Hong Kong *via* Cardiff. Then I returned to my solitary life until she should be ready for sea, counting the days somewhat wistfully until that time should arrive.

I ought to say that I also went to several churches, including the Abbey and St. Paul's, for the service, but did not enjoy it at all, except the singing. Chapels I somehow felt shy at entering ; they always seemed to me like private places in which a stranger had no business. And I knew absolutely nothing about sailors' institutes, because I never remained in Sailor Town. This excessive shyness is characteristic of sailors—they want a good deal of pressing invitation before they will venture shamefacedly into the very places prepared for them.

Taking it altogether, I was by no means sorry when the time came to go to sea again, although I dreaded much the possibility of getting along with a hard crowd after my last delightful experience. But things turned out much better than I had anticipated. Although there was not a single man on board beside myself that had the slightest Christian sympathies, they were a very good lot of fellows, one only excepted. She was well manned, too, for a modern sailing ship ; six A.B.'s and one ordinary in each watch for a vessel under a thousand tons could not but be considered a good crew, in view of the fact that in my last ship, nearly as heavily rigged, we only had four A.B.'s in a watch and no ordinaries. The composition of the crew as far as nationality was concerned was about the average—*i.e.* one Swede, one Dane, one Finn, two Frenchmen (very unusual this for an English ship), one Alsatian (bo'sun), one Italian, one Mauritius negro, three American negroes, whereof one was an ordinary seaman in my watch and the other two were cook and

steward respectively. The remaining thirteen—
that is, master, three mates, carpenter, two boys
(from the ' Chichester '), one ordinary seaman, and
five A.B.'s—were all British, and all, with the
exception of one gaunt Irishman, in my watch,
excellent seamen. This latter individual, who
disgraced the kindly race from which he sprang,
had one accomplishment, one boast—it was that
of possessing the widest experience of prisons of
any man he had ever met with. And he was
always anxious to sample a new one. Taking him
' by and large ' I do not think it possible to give a
more concise summary of Mr. Michael O'Dwyer's
character than that enunciated by the skipper
when we finally got rid of our shipmate in Hong
Hong : ' You're not fit to carry for ballast.' And
so I leave him. A sprightly little countryman of
his in the starboard watch informed me confiden-
tially that he didn't believe O'Dwyer was an
Irishman at all—that he was just a low down
New York mongrel that hated Ireland, and was
doing his best to bring its people into contempt.

Now although the description of this crew may
not seem very promising to a landsman, they were
really a good lot of fellows on the whole. And

as we had a superlatively excellent skipper, who possessed that genius for command without which no master, however seamanlike, can hope to maintain discipline in a merchant ship, we were really fairly comfortable. But of Christianity there was not a shred, a trace. I had a concertina, and was allowed to sing hymns to it as much as I would, my shipmates seeming to take a good deal of pleasure in listening, but their interest in spiritual matters never went any farther. They never interfered with me in any way, listened quietly whenever I talked of Christ, but there it stopped. And this was not good for me. Had they persecuted me, driven me to the one unfailing recourse for comfort, I should have grown and developed undoubtedly; but their good-humoured toleration and unfailing good-fellowship was enervating, and I gradually grew cold spiritually, began to enjoy a good yarn with them, found myself laughing at the old questionable stories, and coming away with a sense of guilt that made me most wretched. So wretched, in fact, that I was glad to get back to their enlivening company again for relief from the tormenting accusation in my own heart.

Perhaps this peculiar frame of mind will sur-

N

prise many of my readers, but I would like them to remember that I was groping my way unaided by any example or precept except the best of all, that which came from the Word itself. And while on the one hand I was intensely afraid of becoming a hypocrite, on the other my natural love of company and cheerful conversation was continually drawing me away from that quietness of tongue and carefulness of behaviour in which alone I felt I could live as the Lord would have me. And I was also greatly self-tormented. It seemed to me that I could hardly dare to open my mouth in speech without saying something to repent of. To me there were no such things as *little* sins. 'Every idle word'—the giving an account of those idle words hereafter robbed me of my peace, and in sheer despair of getting relief I sought my shipmates' company more and more.

But when standing my trick at the wheel, or taking my turn on the look-out, those two silent hours in the stillness of the tropical night were often periods of fierce conflict, wherein I suffered many things, because I was fighting my supposed foes myself, never having learned the lesson of how to stand still and see the salvation of the Lord.

But one inexpressible comfort was mine. It alone kept me from becoming a prey to religious mania, kept me from despair. It was the absolute unassailable certainty of my salvation. Having once believed the words of the Master, 'My sheep hear my voice, and I know them, and they follow me : and I give unto them eternal life ; and they shall never perish, and no one shall snatch them out of my hand. My Father, which hath given them unto me, is greater than all ; and no one is able to snatch them out of the Father's hand. I and the Father are one,' there was in my mind no further question of salvation involved. The eternal life which had been communicated to me by contact with the Son was what its name implied, imperishable. The matter admitted of no controversy.

The trouble was now the worthy maintenance of the position I held, not for fear of punishment, but from dread of grieving the great loving heart of the Saviour, my Lord and my God. Believe me, these statements are not made controversially. Of theological argument I know nothing. But as far as in me lies I must state, having been granted the golden opportunity to do so, how the whole operation of the Gospel of Jesus Christ struck me without any human teaching at all, solely by steady reading of that volume which I accepted entirely as the Word of the Living God. And I have also found the same unassisted conclusions arrived at by many other seamen who have been in like manner thrown upon their own resources.

Well, to return to the 'Dartmouth.' Highly favoured by the weather, we made a fairly rapid passage to Hong Kong, and very soon after our arrival got rid of the only really unpleasant member of the crew, O'Dwyer. The first Sunday in port a steam launch came puffing alongside at about 10 A.M., flying the Bethel flag. A gentleman mounted the side, and, seeking the skipper, asked his permission for any of the crew who wished to do so to attend service on board a ship in the harbour, giving complete assurance that whoever went would be brought straight back again. Alone of our crowd I accepted the invitation, but I am bound to say that the response from the other ships was little better. A goodly fleet was at anchor there, but the whole number that finally disembarked from the launch on board the Bethel ship was under twenty, about one from each ship I should think, not, of course, counting the war-vessels and steamships at the wharves. We climbed on board and stood shyly in a little group, while our shepherd went aft and held a consultation with the captain. Presently a scowling unkempt second mate ambled forrard, and in a hoarse voice shouted : 'Lay aft an' rig the Church.' One by one out of the fo'csle slouched the dirtiest looking crowd of ruffians I ever saw on board of a ship. Not only were they dirty, but they had been enjoying a free fight on the previous evening, and all of them bore evident marks of the struggle. It must have been nearly half an hour before the quarter-deck was prepared for service, by spreading an awning and draping it with flags, as well as providing some kind of seats. This being done, the ship's crew slouched forrard again, muttering curses, and we saw no more of them.

This reception alone would have gone far to chill the desire for assembling ourselves together in worship under such conditions, even had the ensuing service been of the best and brightest kind. Unhappily, it was anything but that. Somebody read the Church of England service very badly ; no hymns were sung, and when that mournful performance was over, somebody else read a sermon out of a book in even more perfunctory style than the service had been delivered. What wonder, then, that every man there registered a vow that nothing should ever tempt him to come to that ship again. For my part, I avow that I was delighted to get away, and I was filled with indignation at the awful waste of means to do good. I blame nobody ; but it was, to my mind, a serious object lesson in the folly of any man taking up work for which he had no qualification, and in which he evidently showed little interest.

As we were not allowed ashore except on liberty day, I had no other opportunity during our stay of assembling with fellow Christians for prayer and praise. I went ashore with my watch on liberty day, and endeavoured to bring my chum, a slow-witted but wonderfully good-natured Finn, back with me before dark. But he evaded me in some way, and when I met some others of my watchmates and, inquired after him, they told me that he was to be found in Tai-pin-shang, a street which had an unsavoury reputation, worse indeed than I had any idea of. Thither I went to look for him, but only succeeded in getting

HALTING ON THE UPWARD WAY 183

myself into serious trouble with the hordes of evil-looking Chinese of both sexes that were lounging about waiting for drunken sailors to prey upon. I escaped with only the loss of a coat-sleeve, which was torn off by a burly Chinaman who endeavoured to stop me as I fled, faster, I think, than I had ever done before in my life. I had seen enough of Hong Kong, so I made direct for the wharf, where sampans lay for hire. Just as I was about to step into the nearest one—it being almost dark at the time—a white policeman came forward and stopped me. Producing a book, he proceeded to enter my replies to his questions of what ship I belonged to, what was my name, and also the number of the sampan, and the hour and minute of my departure. As this proceeding seemed curious, I asked him why these precautions were taken. He told me that they were absolutely necessary, in view of the fact that the sampan coolies would at any time murder a man for his clothes if they thought they could do so without detection. But so thorough was the system of registration adopted in Hong Kong that any sampan coolie could be found out of the twenty thousand or so that gained some sort of a livelihood in this way. I thanked him and started, but admit that I kept a wary eye upon the movements of my boatmen.

I got on board all right and very quickly. The mate greeted me with a coarse joke as I came over the rail, and inquired after my shipmates. But I had no information to give him. Moreover, I was anxious to escape from his peculiar chaff. So as soon as I could in civility I fled forrard and turned in to enjoy a splendid night's rest. Next morning my watchmates all turned up, looking as if the store of robust health they had accumulated during the preceding four months had not only been dissipated, but a heavy overdraft been made upon the future. Two days after we left for Manila in ballast to load hemp for home.

We had a stormy passage across against the full force of the S.W. monsoon, and all my shipmates were very miserable. They were unable to find solace in anything but a recital of their adventures in Hong Kong, and this they indulged themselves with regularly at every meal-time for at least a month. But it would be impossible for me to give here the faintest idea of their conversation, and I am sure that if any of them could have seen a verbatim report of it they would have felt disgusted with themselves. That, however, is one of the regular conditions of fo'csle life, which should always be reckoned with by those who labour for the moral elevation of the sailor.

In Hong Kong we had shipped two men, one to replace O'Dwyer and one to work his passage home, both very nice fellows. But my heart went out to the first one, a tall gentlemanly Yankee from Vermont, who might, I think, have risen to any height he chose, for he had great abilities. But having run through his patrimony at a furious rate, he had as a last resource taken to the sea. American ships were too much for him, he said : the grub was all right, but the nigger-driving he couldn't stand. English vessels just suited him, for he could put up with a good deal of starvation, Red Indian fashion, if he only could at regular intervals have an enormous feed. But steady, persistent hard work he could not, would not, do. His story was a sad one. Left master of a fine farm near the Canadian border of Vermont, he found life dull, and having during his various visits to the eastern cities acquired a keen thirst for intoxicants, he took that method of enlivening himself. It was not easy, for Vermont was strictly a Prohibition State—no liquor was obtainable except under a doctor's order. So he used to hitch up his splendid team of horses and drive I don't know how many miles into Canada, returning laden with cases of champagne and brandy. Then, calling to his aid other young fellows like-minded, they would enter upon a debauch which lasted until the drink was all gone.

This went on until he had spent all, in spite of the loving remonstrances of his friends, of the loss of his sweetheart, who sensibly enough refused to marry him unless he reformed. And now he was an A.B. on board the 'Dartmouth,' in the full vigour of manhood and intelligence, but without a single aspiration or care for the future.

He and I became very close friends, and I naturally tried my universal remedy on him. But he was as hard as the nether millstone. He never scoffed at me, never spoke harshly of God or the Bible, but he said that he was certain, from his experience of professing Christians, that not one of them was anything but the worst kind of hypocrite, only assuming a sanctimonious air of religion for selfish purposes. He showed me letters from friends of both sexes, full of the most tender expressions of concern for him, offering to do all that was possible to them for his reclamation. And having read them I told him that it was impossible for me to understand his attitude of mind. He did not attempt to explain or defend it, and I was obliged to believe that the only reason for it was the old one, *i.e.* that sin was so pleasant to him that he was willing to go any length, suffer any consequences, rather than abandon it or have it taken away from him. It was grievous in the extreme, for he was one of the dearest fellows I have ever met.

And now, having outrun my space for this chapter, I must close it in a few words. The passage home was uneventful and comfortable. Too comfortable perhaps for me, for I was conscious of a distinct relaxation of moral fibre, there being no opposition and no fellowship in spiritual matters. I still pursued my studies in navigation, and had the satisfaction not only of teaching others but of 'passing' for second mate myself a fortnight after I left the ship. In fact, on the arrival home of the 'Dartmouth' I entered upon a totally new phase of my life.

CHAPTER X

A LONG-FELT WANT SUPPLIED

UPON leaving the 'Dartmouth,' which it is my peculiar pride and pleasure to remember that I did with the goodwill of everyone on board, I somewhat timidly interviewed the 'old man.' He was very taciturn, and seldom came into personal contact with any of the foremast hands, yet, as I have said, he made his authority so thoroughly felt that the vessel was more perfectly disciplined than any merchant ship I have ever sailed in. But I could not help feeling that, since he had not spoken a hundred words to me during the voyage of nearly twelve months, he would not be very likely to respond graciously to the question I was about to put to him. But it was essential that I should obtain what I wanted from him, as otherwise I could not do what I had set my heart upon, viz. go up for examination by the Board of Trade officials for the qualifications of a second mate.

Unless I had a personal reference from my last master, I would not be permitted to enter the lists at all, so I braced up and tackled the stern old gentleman, finding to my intense surprise and gratification that he was most gracious towards me. He gave me a really splendid testimonial, telling me that he had kept his eye upon me all the voyage. The sea-stained and weather-worn old document is before me now as I write, but I will not quote it for fear of being accused of vanity.

The examination I found ridiculously easy, although I had dreaded it much, and with my creamy new certificate in my pocket I felt quite proud. Indeed, about this time I was very happy. I was, as I have said before, in the early twenties, and for the first time in my life I fell in love. Better still, my affection was returned, and the girl of my choice did not think worse of me, but better, because I was 'very religious.' Visions of a home of my own, of someone there while I was at sea who would pray for me and long for my return, blossomed before my mental vision, and I went in for castle-building extensively. It is impossible to say what this new development meant to me. To one so long alone in the world as I had been, without one beloved object upon whom to pour out the treasures of a naturally warm heart, the prospect of possessing that object was entrancing. No thought of what the weary separations might mean to her troubled me. Selfishly, I am afraid, I only thought of the joy of finding a natural outlet for long pent-up affection, of having a lode-star somewhere on earth, some person who would think about me and be grieved at my death if that should happen.

Yes, I was very happy. Not even the disconcerting fact that I was compelled to go to sea again as an A.B. had power to make me miserable. Really I had expected that, for no one knew better than I did how very difficult it was for a friendless young officer to get a ship in London. But I did hope that perhaps in some far-away port I might get a ship as second mate and prevail upon my skipper to let me go. So, in this hope, I got a ship bound for new Zealand again, a most beautiful looking vessel of about 800 tons register, and, much to my gratification, had two of my old shipmates of the 'Dartmouth' ship with me. I cannot name my new vessel, for her owner is still alive, and I would not like to hurt his feelings by the hard things I must presently say about her.

Besides, he (the owner) is, I know, a very good Christian man, and it would grieve him much to know how utterly Godless was the life on board any one of his ships. The sailing day arrived, and I felt for the first time the pain of parting with one of the opposite sex, who, in the three weeks of our acquaintance, had become very dear to me. But my pain was, I know, very light compared with hers. We were both friendless youngsters, but I realised afterwards how much harder was her lot than mine, how weary her life was cooped up in a stuffy work-room in the city of London, with only the hope of meeting me again to look forward to. My sorrow was brief, for many things combined to drive it away, and I had what to me was a great boon, somebody at home to think of, to plan for, and to look forward to meeting again.

We left the South-West India Docks in fine fettle, with, for a wonder, a sober crew, and before we had been twelve hours out of dock were pulling together as if we had been shipmates all our lives—

so much so that two days after, when we encountered that tremendous squall in which the 'Eurydice' foundered (we were only a few miles to leeward of her when she capsized) we made light of it, handling the vessel like a yacht. We had half-a-dozen passengers on board—a lady going out to join her husband, with her little girl, a Yankee traveller in the saloon, and four second-class passengers, who lived in the apprentices' house forrard. All looked forward to making a speedy, comfortable passage, the vessel being fast and handy in smooth water. But, oh! when she first met with a moderately heavy sea! Then she revealed herself to us in all her innate brutality. I really think that she had almost every vice that a ship can have. Yet it may have been her cargo, for she was deeply laden with general merchandise, of which at least 400 tons was iron, mostly in the shape of rods and wire, which of course made her unkindly in a sea-way.

In addition to the discomfort of the ship herself, the skipper and the mate both drank to excess in bad weather, and often when all hands had been called to shorten sail the watch that should have gone below were kept standing about in the deep water on deck, not daring to go below until told, yet knowing very well that there was no earthly reason why they should be kept there. At other times I have seen the watch below all standing ready clad in oilskin just inside the fo'csle door expecting to be called upon to shorten sail while the vessel, pressed far beyond what she could safely bear, was wallowing along through an awful sea, burying herself under it, and the skipper and mate, both rolling drunk, were tumbling about inside the cabin.

Yet this experience was not bad for me. It drove me back again to my ever-faithful comforter, it made me pray to be spared for the sake of the watching one at home, and even when I stood at the wheel, peering into a compass that had lost its polarity, trying in vain to 'feel' through the asinine complications of the patent steering-gear how she wanted helm, and unable to fix any other guide for my course than the feel of the wind in the pitchy blackness of the night, I often felt quite cheerful. But it was always an anxious time, and although there was no sense of religion as far as I could see on board, there was far less profanity and filth in the fo'csle than customary.

o

There was only one man who was inclined to make things unpleasant in the fo'csle by his roughness and wickedness generally, and he, strangely enough, was a Scotchman from the far North, a great raw-boned, shoulder-of-mutton fisted fellow that ought to have been a Cameronian Elder. Unlike O'Dwyer of the 'Dartmouth,' though, Angus was a splendid seaman and a hard worker, and I think only his natural desire to rule made him cantankerous. At any rate, he was exceedingly hard upon my poor, easy-going Finn chum, who, as I said before, had followed me out of the 'Dartmouth.' No doubt poor Johnny was aggravatingly deliberate in his movements, no doubt the mild pathetic look in his light blue eyes and his feeble command of English were somewhat trying; but these things, coupled with his extraordinary amiability and his staunch friendship for me, made me feel any indignity put upon him more than if it had been put upon myself.

Therefore, one memorable afternoon (to me), when I had come into the fo'csle on some errand, and I heard Angus berating poor Johnny in no measured tones, I ventured to tell the big Scotchman that he ought to be ashamed of himself for thus taking advantage of a harmless fellow who, but that he was a little slow, was as good a man as any in the ship. My remarks transformed Angus into a furious demon who thirsted for my blood, but singularly enough he did not immediately attack me. He only invited me to come outside and be pounded into a jelly. Then I told him that I was anything but a fighting man, even had the conditions of warfare been equal. I told him that I knew he could probably break all my bones with his left hand tied behind him. But that knowledge would never prevent me from saying a word for the right, and I felt sure that if he would only give the matter his calm consideration he would agree with me that his behaviour towards Johnny was utterly unworthy of a big brave man. For a few minutes I thought he would break a blood-vessel, he was so enraged ; then he cooled down slightly and went to a seat, with his head between his hands. And thenceforward, although Angus and I were never very intimate, he and Johnny were firm friends. They sailed together for years, until the vessel in which they were coming home was lost, and poor John was drowned. But that story is too long to be told here, involving as it does a recital of self-sacrificing love that has never been excelled in any fiction.

Bad as the behaviour of the vessel always was, we did not suffer the full measure of her iniquity until we were well within the stormy region between the Cape and Australia known to seamen as the 'Easting.' Then it was found necessary for the safety of the ship to build a barricade of two-inch planks right across the front of the poop, for the enormous masses of water that kept bursting over all threatened to gut the whole of the officers' and passengers' quarters. Running before the westerly gale and following sea she was like a half-tide rock, and for six weeks we lived in oil-skins and sea-boots, while the slimy sea-grass grew thickly upon her decks, owing to the incessant wash of the sea over her.

In the fo'csle we did not discuss the matter much, but every one of us felt that we were being balanced upon the very edge of death, and the drunkenness of the skipper made matters so much worse for us. At last, on Easter Sunday, when the gale was at its height, it was manifest that, firstly, the amount of sail she could carry would not suffice to keep her ahead of the sea any longer; secondly, that the operation of 'heaving-to,' while attended with the most terrible danger, must be performed ; and, lastly, that in all human probability before another twenty-four hours had passed we should all have disappeared from mortal ken, like one of the bursting bubbles on the foam crests around.   At 10 A.M. all hands were called and ordered to stand by for 'heaving-to.'   Now this term, though highly technical, is, I think, susceptible of explanation to landsmen.   It means that, as the ship is built to breast the sea, her safest position in a gale is with her bows pointing as nearly in the direction from which wind and sea are coming as possible, for she then rises to meet the waves, whereas when the waves are overtaking her the stern has a tendency to cower down before them and let them rage over the deck, doing dreadful damage.   But after a ship has been running before wind and sea until both have risen to a fearful height, it becomes a task of great danger and difficulty to 'heave-to '—that is, to turn her round to face the elements she has been fleeing from.

First of all, it means the reduction of sail to

almost nothing, which, as it reduces the vessel's speed, is in itself a serious danger, as the halting vessel may be overwhelmed. Next, in the actual process of turning the ship round she must of necessity be for a brief space broadside on to those tremendous waves, presenting her most vulnerable part to their awful attack. And then much depends upon the seaworthy qualities of the vessel herself. Some ships seem never to have got upon intimate terms with the sea—they actually court attack and consequent injury; while others will brave and weather the fiercest storms with impunity, as if they were as privileged citizens of the sea as the birds and fish. Our ship belonged to the former hapless class, so that when we took our stations it was with the gloomiest apprehension that we viewed the task before us. As we waited the sky cleared a little, and the 'old man,' catching at the smallest hope, 'hung on,' to see if the weather was really going to be finer. But while we stood watching the incessant onslaught of those moun- tainous seas, there suddenly came howling out from the westward an awful squall laden with snow. The winds seemed to redouble in violence, the whole air was obscured by the fast falling flakes, and as the miserable ship, like an over-driven horse, tried to stagger forward, three vast seas leapt on board at once, one over the taffrail and one over each side. I was on the fo'csle head, stationed there at the fore-topmast staysail sheet with the other old shipmate from the 'Dartmouth,' a nice fellow, but profligate and Godless to the last degree. In silence we gazed upon the dreadful scene. Out of that whirling waste of white only the three masts emerged; all the rest of the ship was hidden from view. And beneath our feet we felt that the sorely-tried hull was quivering as if in a death throe under the mighty weight of water. While we gazed, Bill drew nearer to me and said : ' I wish I'd lived a better life. It's awful to look death in the face like this, and feel that you ain't ready to go. You look all right. How do you feel ?' The responsibility of answering was great, but gratefully I record that at that dread moment my only feeling was one of triumph. And I said : ' Bill, it's one of the blessings that God gives to any poor weak mortal that leans on Him at all times, that when the hour of trial comes the necessity for worrying about anything but one's immediate duty is taken away. There's no thought of how much or how little one has done to justify the favour of God, but only the deep secure sense of being immortal, of having just depended upon the unbreakable word of the Father.' He was silent for a minute, and then he replied : ' Well, if ever I get out of this alive, I bet I'll be a different man. I feel horrible frightened to meet God like I am.' Now this man was anything but a namby-pamby fellow who was likely to be swayed by fear ; on the contrary, he was brave and reckless to the last degree, besides being a splendid seaman. But standing there quietly and looking upon what seemed the inevitable destruction of the ship, and knowing that if she foundered there would be not the remotest hope of any of her crew surviving, was too much even for his seasoned nerves, and he spoke as I have said.

Yet I admit that I had not the slightest faith in any permanent change being wrought in the man. Much bitter experience of my own had convinced me that conversions as the result of fear are the rarest exceptions to a universal rule of the Gospel's winning by love. So I told him that I knew he was quite sincere now, and I earnestly hoped that when, if ever, he had the opportunity of showing his readiness to be a Christian in fine weather he would remember his promise. There and then he took the most solemn oath that for the future he would serve God and Him only, if his life were but spared this once—which did not impress me in the least, knowing full well, as I did, that if he would break his promise to God he would break any oath also.

The water subsided from the deck, revealing a wretched state of affairs. The bulwarks had burst outwards for the greater part of the ship's length on both sides, the massive breakwater built across the front of the cabin had completely disappeared, and the handsome teak front of the saloon was all gone also, leaving only the barren iron skeleton and showing the saloon full of water, which (we found afterwards) was pouring down in floods through the grating of the lazaretto to the store-room below. But for the moment nothing could be done to repair damages. It was evident that the ship would not 'run' any longer, so the order was given to lower the top sails and 'spill' them (quiet them by means of special gear for that purpose worked from the deck); and as soon as that was done the skipper, watching for a time when a heavier sea than usual had rolled past, the ninth wave, sang out : 'Hold on, everybody,' and put the helm down. Round she came in the great creaming valley between two vast combers, and all hands watched in breathless suspense to see her pass the danger point. She reached it, waited, lurched up against the shoulder of the toppling green mountain, and, with a shudder like that of a dying animal, allowed it to overwhelm her. Yet she was so staunchly built that nothing more important than deck fittings was carried away, and she rose again, bowing the sea, and, for the time at any rate, safe. But throughout the next forty-eight hours her behaviour was even more terrifying than when she was running. She would roll to windward and allow an enormous sea to tumble on board, then over, over she would go to leeward, until not only the rail, but even the sheer-poles of the rigging were under water, then back again, and so on continually. There was not a dry corner in the ship, and the poor lady with her little child in the aftercabin sat in an upper bunk watching the turbid waters lash to and fro in her berth, destroying all her belongings, and compelling her to believe that the ship was sinking.

By the mercy of God the wind eased and the sea went down, so that we were able once more to make sail and in some small measure repair damages. And for the rest of the passage the weather was sufficiently good to enable us to make an ordinary passage. As I had expected, Bill's fit of righteousness lasted but a few days. It was most curious to see how shamefacedly he avoided me, as if my opinion or even censure, had I dared or felt inclined to give it to him, could have been of any moment. Only a common instance, I suppose, of how prone we all are to fear the creature more than the Creator, to value the seen above the Unseen.

Upon our arrival in Port Lyttelton I was most fortunate in finding that a dear friend of Port Chalmers days was in the neighbourhood, in the position of dispenser to Christchurch Hospital. In his pleasant company I spent some happy hours, renewing my memories of that best of all times in my life. And then one morning my skipper sent for me and told me that a large ship in the harbour was in need of a second mate, and that he had recommended me for the post. But, he added, as I was bettering myself, and as he would have to pay at least 30s. per month more for a substitute for me than I was receiving, he could not give me any of my wages. I pleaded with him to let me have a little, representing to him that there were several necessaries I must have on taking up my new position, but he would not hear me. He did not want me to go, he said, but if I went those were the conditions. So I went, and lost as hardly earned a sum of 10l. as ever I had been entitled to in my life. I parted with my shipmates with real regret, for I had been happy with all of them. Especially gratifying was my parting with big Angus, who told me in a shame-faced way that my chum John, the Finn, should never want for a friend as long as he was alive. And thus with the good wishes of everybody I left the fo'csle for the quarter-deck.

Here I feel that a new chapter ought to begin, but alas I am reminded that I am now on the last instalment of the serial portion of this story, and I must of necessity go on to say as much as I can of the new condition of things in the small space still left to me.

At my first meeting with my new skipper I felt a thrill of delight. He was an elderly Orkney man named Seator, overflowing with benevolence, a sincere Christian and an excellent seaman. His reception of me was so kind that I was almost unable to say a word for emotion. As if I had been an officer of ripe experience instead of a foremast hand just promoted, he made me welcome, spoke to me man fashion, and told me that he was sure I should do well. And my first impressions of George Traill Seator were, I rejoice to say, not only abundantly confirmed, but they were deepened and strengthened the longer I knew him. He was a man whom I am proud to have lived to know.

The ship, which was an old one belonging to Messrs. Shaw Savill & Co., had been absent from England over two years, and still retained her original crew, who were nearly all Britons. She was emphatically a happy ship.

At this time she was chartered by the New Zealand Government to convey a cargo of railway material to Adelaide, and my first duty on board was to superintend the stowage of railway wagons and locomotives, a task which pleased me very much. And when at last she was ready for sea and shifted out into the bay from the wharf, the amiable old mate had a serious fall which laid him up, and I was by force of circumstances compelled to act as chief officer. But this gave me no concern, for the confidence reposed in me by the master, the knowledge that I was not being watched in the hope of fault-finding, helped me marvellously, as it would have been a proof of the most utter incompetency on my part had I failed to rise to so favourable an occasion.

A most peculiar state of affairs prevailed on board, such as I suppose no other merchant ship has ever known. All the ship's company were teetotallers, and several of them were Good Templars. And one of the A.B.s, who had held high office in the Order, suggested that we should have a Lodge on board, since we were thirty strong. The skipper gladly agreed, and a dispensation being received from the Grand Lodge of Australasia (I believe), the 'Bulwark of England' Lodge was duly constituted. We purchased a second-hand set of regalia, one of the A.B.s became W.C.T., the skipper was chaplain, the mate treasurer, myself secretary, and so on. Besides being great fun, the serious side worked exceedingly well, and there was no loss of disciplinary force at all. And in addition to the Lodge meetings in the saloon, we had most pleasant services conducted by the good old man. Is it any wonder therefore that she was a happy ship?

Unhappily these pleasant, almost ideal, conditions soon came to a close. In the nature of things our trip to Adelaide could not last very long, and a few days after our arrival there the news reached us that as soon as the cargo was discharged the ship was to pay off and be put up for sale. In the meantime the good folk of Port Adelaide were mightily interested in this unique Lodge of ours, and the local Lodges vied with each other to try and make our visit pleasant. Thus we made troops of friends, and when the time came to pay off and distribute the ship's company to the four winds there was much genuine regret. Our Lodge was formally dissolved, the regalia were given away, and the members thereof departed each unto his own place, with three exceptions, the captain, the steward, and myself, who still lived on board the old ship to take care of her until a purchaser should come along. It was a very pleasant life indeed, but of course it could not last long in the nature of things. I was the first of the trio to leave. The master of a local barque came on board ne day in a mighty hurry desiring to ship me as mate of his vessel, which was ordered on a foreign voyage, and was compelled to carry a man with at least an English second mate's certificate. My old skipper was kindness itself, as usual. He said he was extremely loth to lose my company, but it was a step up the ladder for me to go as mate, and I had better take the offer. I did so, and in three hours from the time that it was made I was standing on her fo'csle, being towed down the river, bound to New Caledonia.

And now it becomes my painful duty to close this chapter, and with it the serial portion of this story. In the further five chapters which I have to write in order to complete my work, I have a record of ups and downs to make of greater variety than anything that has gone before— variety both in worldly and spiritual matters. In fact, this period of my life has been far more filled with interesting incidents than any other, I think, unless I except the whaling cruise. Whether I shall be able to relate them interestingly is another thing. I can only promise to those who have read thus far and been interested that I will do my best in order that they shall not be disappointed in the completed book.

CHAPTER XI

A DIP INTO TARTARUS

NOT until my new vessel was fairly out upon the bosom of St. Vincent Gulf did I have time to meditate upon this sudden change in my condition, for I was kept pretty busy preparing the ship for the voyage, setting sail, &c. When breathing time came, I saw that, elated as I had been at the sudden elevation in my position, there were all the elements of trouble in it. The master was a young, nervous man, somewhat disposed to stand upon what little dignity he could muster, but himself placed rather awkwardly for so doing. His father, who was an old sea captain but had long ago retired from active service, was also owner of the vessel and had taken it into his head to come this trip with us. The son, having been newly married, had brought his wife with him, and the three of them used up all the accommodation that the small lower cabin held. Therefore I was

obliged to share the second mate's berth, a little
dog-hole of a place, not really large enough for
one, not one quarter as large as my comfortable
room on board my last ship. And as I had
learned to value very highly the privilege of
privacy, I felt somewhat sick at so suddenly losing
it again. Moreover, the owner treated his son
very much like a big boy, which the latter felt
keenly but dared not resent. So he looked,
naturally enough, as if he would like to pass on
his father's treatment of him to someone beneath
him. And I saw at once that the someone must
needs be me unless I were able to hold my own,
for the second mate was an elderly Swede, who
had been in the ship for years and combined in
himself the various offices of bosun, sailmaker,
and watchkeeper; in fact he could and would do
anything that was required—a wonderfully valuable man to have on board such a vessel, and one
who knew his worth, nor was likely to let himself
be imposed upon. All the crew were seasoned
colonial coasting sailors, who would not put up
with any 'nonsense,' as they called it, from anybody; so *they* must be left alone.

Now I was not really needed on board at all,

having only been engaged for legal purposes, and the knowledge that 7*l.* per month was being expended for no adequate return, as they thought, was not comforting. But there I was, and there I had to remain, making the best of my fifth-wheel-of-a-coach feeling that I could. For the first few days, the skipper's young wife being very sick, much of his time was taken up with her, and I was left to keep my regular watch unmolested, for the old gentleman treated me with a peculiarly distant courtesy that, while it was puzzling, was not altogether unpleasant. When, however, the lady began to get about, the old gentleman continually worried his son, who in turn worried me, interfering in my work of looking after the ship, making and trimming sail, &c., and only let me have peace in the matter of my navigation.

Here also of Christianity there did not appear to be a trace. They were all decent folk enough and well behaved, as sailors usually are when the skipper carries his wife ; but that was all. More than that, they were like a family party with an unwelcome stranger in the house, which, after the homeliness of my last ship, was hard for me, the said stranger, to bear. So that, before a week had elapsed, I was most weary of my lot, and would gladly have exchanged places with one of the chaps forrard. It was just as much as I could do to keep myself from being imposed upon and treated boy-fashion, but I did manage it somehow.

We had a very fine passage north to Noumea, making a splendid landfall about midday and receiving a French pilot on board, outside the great fringing coral reef that guards the island. But we found, after we had entered between the two pier-like masses of foam which marked the gap between the reefs, that we must tack up into the harbour. There was scant room, so our tacks were short ; but as the little barque was easily handled, that did not matter. At the fourth tack, I being on the fo'csle in my place, the skipper, pilot, and second mate all aft, conning the ship as I thought, I saw she was heading direct for a bluff headland, from the base of which a long reef-spur ran straight out to meet us—the water being so smooth there were no breakers to mark it, but the discoloration of the otherwise bright blue water was quite sufficient to show its position. Right on she was held towards it, while I kept casting anxious glances aft to see if the pilot was awake. The three of them aft seemed to be on the alert, but at last, when less than her own length separated her from the reef, I could stand it no longer, and, with a frantic wave of my arms, yelled ' Hard up!' The skipper sprang to the assistance of the helmsman, and between them they hove the wheel hard over, feeling as they did so the long terrible grinding of the coral barrier along her side.   Fifteen seconds more and she must have been totally lost, for she would have run butt into the reef at the rate of six or seven knots an hour, while the pilot stood like an image of stone.   It was the only time I ever saw a pilot interfered with in my life, but, my word, it was needed then.

With a feeling of deep content at my heart, I did the necessary work of trimming sail as the vessel sped into the harbour. The skipper came forward, with white drawn face, to ask my version of the incident. And all I could tell him was that it appeared to me as if the pilot had been seized with a momentary suspension of the mental faculties, such as does undoubtedly seize upon men of middle age sometimes at the most critical junctures, often occasioning irreparable loss and suffering. However, we consoled ourselves with the thought that most probably the ship had only suffered the loss of a few sheets of copper from her bilge. Thenceforward we devoted our attention to getting her safely anchored, running well in, past a whole fleet of French warships, into a most secure haven.

Now, since there was nothing more to be done but discharge the cargo, and that work was, by the owner's orders, carried out by the skipper, my position soon became unbearable. I had nothing to do except potter about by myself. The bosun and the men were engaged on the cargo, and I, like a supernumerary for whom there was really no place in the ship, tried most unsuccessfully to reconcile myself to this miserable state of affairs. Except for this, I had nothing to complain of, for my treatment was punctiliously polite. Nevertheless, the unspoken wish that I would take myself off was manifest in every look the other officers gave me. So in a few days I made up my mind that if there was the remotest chance of getting away from this place I would ask for my discharge.

An opportunity soon presented itself. Christmas Day arrived, and in the afternoon I obtained permission to go ashore for a ramble. On my way thither in the boat, I passed a couple of lovely little white schooners of the fascinating model turned out by the Auckland shipbuilders. So beautiful were they that I could have fancied them gentlemen's yachts, had their deck fittings corresponded with their graceful outlines. I noticed also that they both hailed from Noumea. But presently so many strange matters claimed my attention ashore that I forgot all about these pretty schooners for the time.

Noumea lay simmering in the fierce tropical heat, a town where all people slept. Along the deserted thoroughfares I plodded wearily, out into the country, seeking shade and finding only stuffiness. By and by I got back again to the seashore and trudged along the sand with burning feet and aching head, until I found a great rock, beneath whose shadow I lay down and was soon fast asleep. When I woke the sun was setting and there was a delightful feeling of freshness in the air. Reinvigorated, I strolled back into the town, to find that the population was moving again. As I walked through one of the principal streets I was accosted by a huge negro, who leaned against the verandah posts of a pretentious building

across the front of which were painted the words
'George Washington Hotel.'   In unmistakable
American accents he invited me to come in and
rest, telling me that he had 'spotted' me from afar
for an Anglo-Saxon, and saying that he 'guessed
he ran this hotel for the benefit of such members of
that distinguished race as were unfortunate enough
to find themselves stranded in this God-forsaken
hole.'   Not without   some   considerable   mental
qualms did I accept his invitation.   But I realised
that I must either do that or go on board, as I
was hungry, thirsty and weary.   So I turned in
thither and purchased some iced beverage, exceedingly refreshing.   Mine host informed me that
there would be a Christmas dinner on presently, to
which I was heartily welcome, and there would be
several of my countrymen to keep me company.

This was sufficient inducement to me to stay ;
indeed, I was glad of such an opportunity, in spite
of the trouble I had with my conscience about it.
For I had never been inside the doors of a grog-
shop (which, in spite of its magnificent title, was
the true character of this place) since my conversion.   However, I argued myself into it, stifling all
objections that were raised within, and having once

done so, the rest was easy. The company began to arrive, eight stalwart bearded white men, of British and Yankee origin. They were extremely cordial, pressing all manner of fluid hospitality upon me, and mightily disappointed when I refused. They persevered in their attentions, until, after a little more struggle with that sleepless voice within, I consented to take some wine. After that, of course, I could not go, but sat on and listened to some of the most lurid tales of South Sea abominations ever imagined. I wish I could describe the state of my mind. As the stream of awful talk flowed on, I felt I would give anything to be elsewhere ; yet something held me fast—I lacked the courage to flee. I am afraid I lacked also the full desire. And in order to drown the constantly warning voice I took more and more of the wine until I was sufficiently excited to disregard its worrying.

Thus it came about that one of my new-found acquaintances, having ascertained who and what I was, informed me that he was skipper of one of the smart schooners which I had seen at anchor in the harbour, and pointed out a huge Scotchman, sitting opposite, as his mate. He then told me that he wanted a sailing master, his last one having recently died, and he himself knowing no navigation. He was going to run down to the New Hebrides, on a peaceful trading trip, exchanging the usual assortment of valueless trumpery for sandalwood, copra, and pearl-shell, transactions whereby the original outlay would return something like 1,000 per cent. If I would engage to go with him he would pay me 15*l.* per month, and I should lead a gentleman's life. Here was, I dared not say a heaven-sent way out of my troubles, but at all events a lucrative way, and so I gladly accepted. Not, however, without feeling that the step I was taking would be an unblessed one, for, contrary to my usual custom, I did not ask God to prosper me in it. I felt that the attendant circumstances were too doubtful.

I returned on board and went to my bunk, still prayerless and bearing a sense of wrong-doing; but with a feeling that if I was really as wrong as I felt myself to be, I should surely have to bear the result, and a sort of satisfaction at my willingness to pay the penalty demanded. It is a curious frame of mind this, and I have often wondered whether many Christians experience it. To those who have never felt that the central fact of their lives is their realised position as sons and daughters of the Lord God Almighty, these harassing mental difficulties will appear inexplicable, I know; but to anyone who occupies that position they will be as clear as possible, even if they themselves have never stood on quite the same ground. But I humbly conceive that it is the duty of a faithful chronicler to omit nothing essential from his narrative, either from a dread of being misunderstood or not believed, and therefore I must needs set down here, as far as in me lies the ability so to do, what was my mental condition at that time.

When the owner heard my request for my discharge he could scarcely conceal his satisfaction; although, as he had no fault to find, he could not help uttering a few conventional expressions of regret, of which both he and I knew the exact value. So I departed for the shore with my belongings. On the way up to the hotel with them I saw a most sorrowful sight—a string of men and women, the former totally naked, save for a string round the waist serving a peculiar purpose, and another string round the neck bearing a tin

ticket, whereon was stamped a number. The
women had each a single cotton garment, like a
lengthy petticoat, the band buttoned round the
neck, which also bore a ticket. Leaving my clothes
at the hotel, I hastened to follow this forlorn crowd
to their destination—a market place—where, with
due legal form, they were *apprenticed* for three
years, at an average salary of 5*l.* a year and certain
rations of food. To me the whole thing was
utterly undistinguishable from slavery, since it was
evident that these poor bewildered grown-up
children had but the haziest notion of what was
happening to them, where they were going, for
how long, or at what remuneration. And the
pitiful dumb appeal on their faces was hard to bear
the sight of. Indeed, I could not bear it, and
hurried away, full of inarticulate rage at someone,
I knew not whom.

Little time was wasted by my new employer.
Two days afterward I had embarked and taken up
my quarters in the little cabin, duly installed as
sailing master, and looked upon with good-natured
contempt by the gigantic mate. The crew were a
jolly set of Rarotongan Kanakas, full of fun as
kittens, and as smart at their work as heart could

wish. The manner in which they handled the schooner getting under way extorted my utmost admiration, and I had ample leisure to observe them, since I was treated just like a favoured passenger. It gave me a queer feeling, though, to see the French flag floating overhead.

Our run down to Mallicolo was swift and uneventful, the weather being all that could be desired, and but for one thing I should have enjoyed it very much. That one drawback was the behaviour of my two white shipmates; they drank incessantly of 'square' gin, and their sole conversation was a string of blood-curdling blasphemies. Because I could not join them and scarcely opened my mouth they were offended, but presently agreed that I was a poor kind of idiot whom it was perhaps best to let go my own way, so long as I did the work for which they carried me. So I gradually shrank closer and closer into myself, full of self-reproaches for having come, and trying to regain the peace of mind I had lost by acknowledging that I was only receiving my just deserts. But when we reached our first calling-place I saw with suddenly wide-opened eyes what I really had done for myself. I was in a 'blackbirder'—an

officer of one of those hateful vessels that I had
heard described with such wealth of lurid detail
when I was a lad on the Australian coast; and I
remembered the hanging of some of the fiends at
Darlinghurst Gaol for that they were caught red-
handed stealing men.

Then I resolved that, come what might, I
would have no hand in the business, for it would
be a comparatively easy matter to let oneself be
shot, if need be, rather than be an accessory to
such a crime against fellow-men as that; for the
ostensible legality of the whole black business did
not deceive me at all. And after the first trans-
action, when I saw how the childlike ignorance of
those poor savages was traded upon, how the
scoundrelly interpreter prophesied smooth things
to them, painted glowing pictures for them of the
golden career which was opening up for them, I
was absolutely certain that my first impressions
were correct. Of the conditions of life on board,
the debauchery, open and unashamed, the bestial
degradation, I dare not speak more fully. The
plain language in which alone those doings could
be characterised would not only shock but disgust
my readers; and in any case a recital of them, if

permissible, could do little or no good. Therefore I pass swiftly over the six weeks or so spent among the islands—over forty days of horrible nightmare, during which time I was never once able to get away from those sights and sounds for a single day—with a feeling of relief.

Nothing, I think, ever gave me such exquisite pleasure as did the sight of New Caledonia again, for it meant to me the closing of a chapter of horrors in my life that ever since has seemed to belong to some temporary absence in the infernal regions. In that small vessel we brought 204 Kanakas, of both sexes, to Noumea, half of whom were, I do not hesitate to say, as much kidnapped as any Central African natives have ever been by Arabs. Six of them died on the short passage from Tanna to Noumea, and were dropped overboard, amid the piercing wails of their companions; but I thought grimly that they were the fortunate ones, not those left behind. Yet even now I have to admit that those two traders were not as bad as they might have been. They kept faith with me; they did not try to coerce me into aiding them in their infernal traffic; they did, in short, all they could for me, they left me alone. And I hope that for this mercy I was sufficiently grateful.

Perhaps I need not say that I was intensely thankful to find a vessel in Noumea needing a chief mate, a colonial barque, bound to Pam, in the north of the island, to load copper ore for Newcastle, N.S.W. To get on board of her out of that hateful place, and know that I should soon be far away from it and its vilenesses, was inexpressibly gratifying. So when we weighed and began to work round the great island, inside of the barrier reef, through the smooth blue waters of the lagoon, I was so happy that I almost felt as if the price I had paid was not too much. I did not think of the soul-scars I bore, neither did I anticipate the penalty presently to be paid. But it was due, and on the sixth day after leaving Noumea, when we were within about twenty miles of our destination, I took the wheel from the helmsman, telling him to go and get his breakfast. I had only a few minutes before lost my broad-leafed hat, and was wearing a close cloth cap. The sun was blazing down upon me, but I never had heeded that much, so I took no notice. And then suddenly, like a blow from a sledge-hammer, something smote me on the head, and I remembered no more.

When I returned to consciousness, about six hours after, all my strength had gone. Not only so, but it seemed as if my throat had closed up, for when someone placed a pannikin of water to my parched lips I could not swallow. Desire for food was gone, but a consuming thirst remained, which I was unable to satisfy. There I lay, a useless log, but with my mind quite clear and busy with many speculations. Everything going on around me I took note of, and presently heard that the skipper was also ill and as unable to move as I was. But the vessel was taken safely into harbour and anchored, the sole merchant ship there, all the others, some five or six, being French war vessels.

The events of the following days during our stay are all like parts of some fevered dream. So weak that I was unable to lift a hand to my head, I was a prey to the ravages of myriads of the most savage mosquitoes I ever felt, until I used to become delirious, so my shipmates told me. With returning consciousness came such misery that I prayed earnestly for death or relief. And my poor commander was also in evil case. He had just this

Q

advantage over me, that he was delirious the whole time, and so was happily unconscious of how much he was suffering.   The only relief we got from the dreadful insects, mosquitoes, sandflies, and other flies, all bloodthirsty, was to have a fire made in the cabin, whereon cakes of cattle-dung were laid, filling the whole place with a thick yellow smoke, which was more than the vermin could endure. Then, when not one cranny remained free from this pungent acrid vapour, the door and skylights were closed, and we slept, the temperature being about 105°.   We had no proper food and no medicine.   A doctor from the French war vessel 'Lamothe-Picquet' did visit us and give us one dose each, but as it nearly drove what little vitality we had left out of us, we dispensed with his services in future.

Meanwhile the crew, under the second mate, toiled like beavers to get the cargo in so that we might flee.   No attempt was made to stow the bags of copper ore ; they were just dumped down the hatchways in three heaps, and as soon as ever she was considered to be deep enough, the anchor was weighed and she was hauled outside the harbour, where a fresh breeze was blowing pretty continuously. There we waited until the French mail steamer (coaster) came along, and from her we obtained the services of an officer to navigate the vessel across to Newcastle, N.S.W. We sailed immediately, and for two days made fair progress, with a pleasant, steady breeze and fine weather. Then the sky began to look menacing, the wind rose to a gale, and the ill-used ship, her dreadful burden tearing at her bowels, complained in every fibre. Worse and worse grew the weather, higher and higher rose the sea, while I lay helplessly in my dark bunk, listening to the wild uproar above. I heard the masts roll over the side, heard the full sullen roar of the water in the hold and the ceaseless ' clankity-clang-bang ' of the old-fashioned pumps. No one came near me—they were all labouring at utmost strain to try and save the ship. But in face of what I felt to be certain death, I was quite at peace. My vitality was at so low an ebb that life had ceased to seem desirable ; all that I craved for was one cool hand to be laid upon my burning aching head. By and by the steward (who was also cook) remembered me and brought me a little food, such as I was by this time able to swallow. I thanked him feebly, and

in return he overwhelmed me with foul abuse. He
accused me of malingering, of lying there sham-
ming, while better men were being worked to
death. If he were the second mate, he said, he
would drag me on deck by the throat, and I
should work or die.

Even this did not excite any feeling of resentment at the time, for the same reason, I suppose
that the imminent proximity of death gave me no
uneasiness—I was past feeling in that direction.
And in this wretched state I remained for four
days, during which the only kind offices that were
rendered me came from the overworked second
mate—a splendid man, if ever there was one. He
told me that the skipper had not recovered his
reason, but was, like myself, utterly helpless, and,
like me also, reduced to a mere skeleton. He told
me that he had jettisoned about 150 tons of the
ore, but that the water in the ship was washing
over the 'tween-deck beams, and the crew was
nearly done. Also that the French officer had
forgotten his navigation, if indeed he had ever
known any, and that consequently no one knew
where the ship was. If by any means I could
be got on deck and there ascertain the ship's

position, it would put heart into the men, for at present the vessel, with only the three lower masts standing and the stump of the foretopmast, was drifting idly nowhither.

Immediately he said this I sent up a swift petition to the Father that I might be granted sufficient strength and returning memory to do this thing for the sake of my shipmates. And at once I felt sure that I should be able. John dragged me on deck, lashed me in a sitting posture by the taffrail, got my sextant and put it in my trembling hands, and then went below, leaving the skylight wide open, to take the time by the chronometer when I should sing out. The Frenchman stood near, with a sarcastic smile upon his swarthy face. For some time I could not hold the instrument steady enough to catch the sun's image at all, but gradually my shattered nerves quieted a little (I was praying fervently all the while) until I managed to get a good altitude. I called out 'Stop!' but, alas, my voice was like the mew of a just born kitten, and the sight was lost. Then I looked appealingly at the Frenchman, who came up and succeeded in understanding what I wanted. Next shot, he passed the word along, and the altitude and time were obtained.

John got me down below again, and secured me to the cabin table, with my book and paper. Then for nearly two hours I wrestled with the problem of finding the longitude, which under normal conditions would have taken me about ten minutes. By the time it was finished it was nearly noon, and in the same laborious bungling way I got the meridian altitude, and thence the latitude. Thoroughly done, but with a feeling of intense gratitude and triumph, I made the course and distance to Cape Moreton Light eighty miles W.S.W.; and as the wind was fresh from the eastward, it looked hopeful for us reaching there the next morning. I had only just time to give John the course, when I fell back unconscious.

CHAPTER XII

MOUNTAIN AND VALLEY

WHEN I recovered consciousness it was dark and the vessel was rolling steadily, her motion informing me that she was running dead before the wind. I was lying in my bunk, and soon the second mate came down telling me that the wind was holding, and that if my observations were correct we should sight Cape Moreton Light before midnight. Murmuring a dreamy 'Thank God!' I laid myself back again, with a grateful feeling that I was able to raise myself that much without assistance. And between sleeping and waking the rest of the dark hours sped away, until clear above the clang of the pumps and the sullen roar of the flood in the hold a voice reached my ear: 'Light right ahead!' Now I cannot explain how it was, but I felt no intense joy at this, a message of life to all hands. Only a calm sense of satisfaction, as of some blessing coming that had been confidently counted upon, about the arrival of which there had never been any doubt whatever.

When morning broke we were only about six miles seaward of Cape Moreton, but the wind had changed and we could make no further advance towards it. The men were almost at their last ounce of strength, and the water in the hold was gaining ominously. Were we, after all, to sink in sight of port? The second mate dragged me on deck again and secured me in a prominent position where I could see the land. For nearly an hour I sat there, dimly picturing the last scene, when the worn-out vessel and her bravely enduring crew should be swallowed up by the envious sea. Then behind the Cape there rose a long smear of smoke against the bright blue sky, and presently there came rushing seaward one of the fine steamers of the A.S.N. Company. Seeing our inverted ensign, conveying its message of utmost need, she altered her course and came proudly down to us, a veritable sea-angel of deliverance. Halting close alongside, she lowered a boat, and the chief officer came on board. He was horrified to see our desperate condition, especially when he was told that we might sink at any moment. A hawser was soon passed on board of her, and in half an hour from the time we first saw her we were being rapidly towed into safety. Being in haste to reach her destination with the mails, she relinquished us to the first tug that came up, and, with the fervent good wishes of all on board, she turned and sped away northward.

A few hours afterward I was being examined by a sympathetic doctor, who ordered my immediate removal to the hospital for nursing back to strength. The skipper, strangely enough, had recovered his sane consciousness as we towed up the river, but he refused to go into hospital, preferring to get strong again in private lodgings. I bade him good-bye with sincere regret, for we had been companions in suffering, if we had had but little opportunity for knowing each other's qualities. With faithful, sturdy John, the second mate, I parted most reluctantly, nor did I ever hear of him, much less see him, again. But he lingers in my memory still, as fresh and vivid as ever, a simple heroic soul who, without making any profession of serving God, did Him the service He most desires, the service of duty faithfully, unostentatiously done, of doing that which his hand found to do, with all his might, good measure pressed down and running over. He was a much-despised (in British Mercantile Marine circles) 'square head,' a Russian Finn, of Helsingfors, but in all my wanderings I never met a man whom I would rather have at my back in time of utmost need than John Olsen.

Very tenderly the resident surgeon in Brisbane Hospital nursed me back to strength again. And I am afraid I repaid him most ungratefully by taking the first opportunity afforded me in permission to go for a walk, in getting paid off from the ship and booking my passage back to Adelaide. When I told him what I had done he was very angry with me, averring that I was quite unfit to go, and, moreover, that I was most foolish to relinquish my lien on the ship. However, my long detention irked me greatly, and besides I had received a letter from home that made me ache to return. I was still a mere walking skeleton, weighing only some seven stone instead of my then normal weight of eleven, but I was eating voraciously and gaining strength rapidly.

So I went my way on the long passage down south, enjoying the novel sensation of being the guest of the officers and lording it leisurely on board ship to the full. When I arrived in Adelaide I was very nearly fit for sea again, but a kind friend there insisted upon making me welcome to his home, where his mother cared for me most thoughtfully. But I had only been there one day when Captain Seator found me out and came to see me, full of indignation that I had not given him what he was pleased to call the privilege of entertaining me. I had quite a job to explain to him that I could have no idea that he would still be there, but eventually succeeded, and he then devoted all his energies to serving me in another way. He must have taken an immense deal of trouble on my behalf, until one day he came in, beaming, to tell me that he had got me a berth as second mate of the finest ship in the harbour, the 'Harbinger,' belonging then to Messrs. Anderson, Anderson & Co. Oh, how pleased he was! And when he came down to see me off, I am sure no father could have bade his son a more affectionate farewell.

My new ship was by far the most splendid sailing vessel that I had ever seen. And, with the sole exception of her sister, the 'Hesperus,' which was somewhat larger, she remained so, being indeed in every particular all that a seaman could desire for comfort, for beauty, and for speed ; while her size—about 2,500 tons burden—was satisfactory to me, ever fond of a 'great' ship. She was fitted luxuriously for the carriage of passengers, both first and second class, of whom we had, for that passage, about sixty all told. At first I was quite perceptibly overawed by her splendour, but I soon got over that, the captain being an ex-naval officer, who, while he was a strict disciplinarian, was also a most just and kindly man. Moreover, I was delighted with my neat little cabin, where I had the most complete privacy for the first time since leaving Captain Seator. This really struck me as the greatest blessing of all.

I soon fell into the ways of my new ship, which were more orderly and regular than those of any vessel I have ever served in. And I made up my mind that I was going to be very happy, that this was to be the beginning of a new era of prosperity for me; and I thought with calm delight of her who was so patiently waiting at home for me, how this sudden stroke of fortune would enable us to marry and have a home of our own. But presently I found that, although there were so many persons on board, I was without society of any kind. I was prohibited from entertaining passengers in my berth; I might not go forrard into the second cabin; the chief officer was a saturnine elderly man, who associated with nobody, and there was no other member of the crew with whom I might foregather. So I led the life of a hermit, my sole companion a tiny black kitten. It took me some little time to reconcile myself to this new mode of life after my long spell of bustling society, but once the first strangeness of it had worn away, I was not unhappy.

Speaking with all necessary reserve, I should say that there was no attempt made, even in this fine ship, to recognise the existence of God by holding Divine service. It may seem strange that I should have any doubt about it, but the matter is easily explainable. By a special arrangement, I was made to keep the 'eight hours out' every night—that is to say, my only night-sleep was from midnight till 4 A.M.; consequently I always slept in the forenoon from about 9.30 till 11.45, which would be the time when service would be held, if at all. But I am inclined to think that if there had been any, I should have known of it. In any case, I am sure that no religious service ever included the crew. As far as I was concerned, my religious life was fostered by the quiet contemplative existence I led. In the long night watches of the tropics I enjoyed to the full that pleasant communion with the eternities that lies within reach of every sailor, and I was not harassed by constant friction with men totally undisciplined, as is the case in most of our merchant ships. So that, all things being considered, it was a very comfortable, profitable time.

We made a long passage, calling at Cape Town to land some passengers and cargo. I should have noted here that several of our passengers were consumptives who had been ordered a sea voyage, but strangely enough none of them did well. Perhaps the intended remedy had been delayed too long. At any rate, three of the patients left us at Cape Town very ill, and when we arrived at home we heard that all were fully recovered. One young fellow, of gigantic frame, having been very poorly all the passage from Adelaide to the Cape, brightened up so much upon arrival in port that I was quite deceived into imagining that he had taken a sudden turn for the better. But, seeing him painfully climbing the cabin stairs to come on deck the morning after our departure from Table Bay, I asked him how he did, there seemed such an unearthly change again. He replied in short thick gasps that he was 'so much better, the improvement was wonderful.' That evening at eight he died, and his burial next day was a most solemn and affecting ceremony, at which all hands were present, and several of the passengers were moved to tears. But I cannot say whether it had any lasting effect upon anyone's heart, because I do not know.

Then came, for me, one of the most unhappy experiences I have ever met with. We had a quartermaster, an Orkney-man, whose name I have forgotten, but whose features, almost as dark as those of a Hindoo, are branded upon my memory. He was spare in body and languid in his movements, as well as exceedingly silent. And when he was steering he would often loll upon the rim of the wheel in extremely un-seamanlike fashion, for which it was my duty to chide him whenever I saw him doing it. But he never complained or tried to excuse himself in any way, nor did it ever occur to me that there was anything the matter with him. He kept his watch and took his regular trick at the wheel right along, until we arrived in St. Helena and anchored, when he took to his bed. Being very busy, seizing the opportunity to get the ship painted outside, I did not miss him, knew nothing of his being laid up, until, at six that evening, the doctor, in passing, said 'That quartermaster of yours is going home fast.' I was simply horrified, incredulous. But I hastened forrard at once and, apologising for the intrusion, entered the fo'csle, one of those shameful places for the housing of men that are still to be found in many ships, beneath the topgallant fo'csle, and groped my way forward into the eyes of her, where I found him. It was so dark that I could not see his face for some time, the air of the den being unbearably foul in spite of the fact of the hawse-pipes being open; the din of half-drunken men gambling for tobacco and shouting at each other long strings of blasphemous exclamations was deafening, and, in the midst of it all, this man was dying. I spoke in his ear, uttering the Name of comfort very clearly, but he made no sign. I prayed as earnestly as I have ever prayed, before or since, that he might be comforted in his passing, and while I did so, amidst that inferno, he died. Then, turning round to the noisy crowd, I said, 'Boys, your shipmate is dead.' For perhaps a minute there was a silence profound, then a voice somewhere in the gloom cackled 'Ee's a damn sight better off'n I am.' At which there was a round of unmirthful laughter.

The poor body was carried out and laid aside until an undertaker from Jamestown could be procured, since we might not legally dispose of it at sea. The next day the coffin and undertaker arrived, and the corpse was laid in its last receptacle. Pausing for a moment before fitting on the cover, the undertaker asked if anyone would like to take a last look. I, alone of the ship's company, accepted the invitation, and never while I live shall I forget the expression of perfect peace on those worn features. Since then I have only twice looked upon the face of the dead, once upon the face of my own dear little son, but even his calm features did not wear such a look of absolute content as did those of that long-suffering quartermaster.

Being in charge of the ship during the absence of the captain and mate, I could not attend the funeral; but I thought little of that, being even then exceedingly averse to the notion of confounding the cast-off house of the departed one with that which had inhabited it, and regarding the dead body as nothing more or less than any other piece of inanimate matter. When the funeral party returned on board we weighed and put to sea, and from thence homeward had a most pleasant, though slow,

R

passage, the whole period from Adelaide being 130 days.

When we were entering the dock the ship's husband came on board and formally complimented the mate and myself upon the smart appearance of the ship. This emboldened me to ask him whether I might hope to be retained in the Company's service, supposing that the captain was willing. He shook his head, saying 'You see, we have so many of our own young officers to provide for that we are unable to employ outsiders except in such a case as your own, where a promotion abroad makes a vacancy. Have you a first mate's certificate?' I admitted that I had not but felt sure of getting one upon going up for examination, as I proposed doing. 'Well,' he replied, 'in any case, we couldn't take you as second mate, in a ship like this, without a first mate's certificate. If you pass, you can come and see if there's any chance.' I felt that it was hopeless, but I vowed that I would do so.

With the rest of the crew I was discharged, receiving from the captain an excellent testimonial, and then did what most people would call a mad thing: I got married. 'What!' you will say, 'with no prospects, at such an age, and only the few pounds earned within the last four months at your disposal?' Yes; and while admitting fully the unwisdom of the act, from a worldly point of view, I plead my heart-hunger for a *home*, for some central point to which I might look forward in all my journeying, an anchorage whereto I might return and be heartily welcome for myself alone. I cannot say what I would like upon this topic, but I do ask you, my reader, to try and imagine how you would feel if you had never known the delights of a *home*, at the prospect of obtaining one of your own, however humble. But why should I make excuses for this rash act? Much suffering ensued, it is true; but, looking back over the weary years that have elapsed since that Monday morning when we two friendless youngsters bound ourselves to each other in Marylebone Church, I say boldly that if it were again to do, I would do it and rejoice. Yes, I am impenitent, and she, who has suffered with me, is likewise unrepentant. Is it necessary to say that we were very happy? We had one small room, in which the furniture was not our own, and for which we paid the magnificent sum of five shillings per week. And we refused to look ahead. We knew that we could get no comfort by doing that, so we made the present provide us with all the satisfaction we craved. Such a little of the joy of human life we had, but how we did appreciate it! Then came the sorrow. I passed for chief mate as easily as I had done for second, and immediately went down to my old ship, only to find a second mate already on duty, a mere lad, just out of his time. And I turned away, sick at heart; for I knew that now it was the longest of odds against me getting a berth as officer, especially as my little store of sovereigns had dwindled to only two or three.

And, strange to say, that fatal diffidence of mine was now worse than ever. I fought a terrible battle with myself every time I went on board a ship to ask for a berth. When I was answered with what seemed to be the universal 'No,' I shrank away like a whipped dog. To me, as to few men, I believe, those wonderful words of Longfellow appeal:

> Who amid their wants and woes
> Hear the sound of doors that close,
> And of feet that pass them by;
> Grown familiar with disfavour,
> Grown familiar with the savour
> Of the bread by which men die![1]

Oh, those weary dock tramps! day after day

[1] *Legend Beautiful.*

returning with that sickening certainty that soon I *must* go, in whatever capacity. And the heavens above me seemed as brass : I got no reassurance of comfort there. I felt rebellious, I do not deny it. Again and again I asked myself, 'What have I done to deserve this at the hands of the Lord ? Is this the price that he demands for my few days of happiness ?' At last, when not one penny remained, I shipped as A.B. in a big Liverpool ship bound to Calcutta, and when I returned home and told my young wife what I had done, she sat rigid and white as if turned into stone, until, with a moan like a wounded animal, she sank back upon the floor and Nature relieved her with some kindly tears.

The bitterest pang that I now had to endure was that, in addition to my absence, my wife would have to bear the pinch of poverty. My wages were now 3*l.* a month, so that my wife's income was about 8*s.* per week. Of course, she would have to work, and we could only hope that work would always be obtainable. But she bore up most bravely after the first shock had passed, and saw me off dry-eyed ; while I, with a hundred conflicting emotions tearing at my heart, was so busy that I had barely time to wave a last good-bye. Fortunately for me, there was no time to dwell upon my sorrows. Out of a crew of twenty A.B.s, only four were fit for work, the rest being all more or less drunk ; so, as always happens, the few sober ones were almost worked to death trying to make up for their shipmates' deficiencies ; and, much to my disgust, we did not anchor at Gravesend so as to get matters a little bit ship-shape before going to sea, but went straight on, towing as far as Beachy Head before the tug left us to our own devices.

By that time I had found out the kind of crowd I was condemned to live with, for probably four months. Out of nineteen, there were only four who could be spoken to at all with any prospect of a decent answer, and even those four were overborne by the weight of their evil ship-mates. The skipper, however, was a most godly man, full of sincere love for the Lord and his fellow-men. Unhappily, he did not possess that instinct of command also which would have enabled him to make his ship as happy as the 'West York.' And whether it was that he was getting too old for his post, or that his vitality was too much enfeebled, I do not know, but with much regret I have to say that he was lacking in that most essential quality of a seaman, courage. This, of course, could not be hidden from the crew when the first gale was encountered, and thenceforward his authority over them was a thing of naught. But I am getting along too fast.

We had very good weather down Channel, but tediously unfavourable winds, which gave us much work tacking ship. And during this irksome time I found that an elderly seaman whom I had been able to do a small favour to at the shipping office, was long past his work. He was very willing, but his physical powers were gone. Only fifty-eight years of age too; but people ashore little dream how fearfully hard is the wear of the ordinary merchant seaman's life. Occasionally one does find a hale old skipper, but a hale old seaman, hardly ever. The bad food, bad air of the fo'csle, vicissitudes of climate and sudden severe strain alternating with times of great relaxation are all unfavourable to longevity or sustained good health, even without the usual recurrence of debauch on being paid off. This poor old chap was therefore on his last legs, and in addition he had been sleeping about the streets, turned out of the sailors' home as being unable to pay, and not being a sufficiently promising subject for the interested charity of the boarding master, who will often shelter a 'cast-out' from the home for the sake of the advance note he will presently receive. We were in the same watch, and, seeing that his mind was favourably inclined toward me, I took the opportunity of having a little friendly chat with him upon eternal matters. Not entirely unselfish, I am afraid, for it took my mind off my own sorrow. But he would hear nothing about Christ, the Friend—the mere mention of the blessed Name made him furiously angry. Nor would he vouchsafe me one single word of explanation of this strange mental attitude. Therefore I was compelled to confine myself to conversation about other matters, and to letting him tell me his sorrowful story.

On Saturday afternoon the wind veered a little in our favour and we made all sail, but in less than an hour afterwards the weather worsened so much that all hands were called to shorten sail. And just at the close of the work the old seaman Wilson, although he had been forbidden by the mate to go aloft, went needlessly up to do some trivial task on the foremast. I shouted to him to come down, that I would do the job; but he either could not hear or would not heed, and before I had finished the task I was upon, he fell close by my side, upon his head, on the deck. I stooped to raise him, but he was quite dead. He was carried aft and sewn up by the sailmaker, ready for burial next morning.

That was an affecting scene, for the old captain was deeply moved, and not only read the Burial Service but pleaded most earnestly and pathetically over the dead body with his men that they would take this solemn warning. And when afterwards the bell sounded for church in the saloon no one was absent that could possibly come. Yet I date my being ' sent to Coventry ' by my shipmates from that morning ; for when the first hymn was given out I raised the tune, and this simple act of mine seemed to set them all against me, aided, as it doubtless was, by the old gentleman's asking me if I would select the hymns in future. When we got forrard again, there was much scurrilous talk at my expense, and all the good effect that appeared to have been produced by the solemn scene of the morning had entirely vanished.

Thenceforward matters got worse and worse, until I was driven to live as much as possible by myself, only coming into the fo'csle when I was obliged to. And the discipline of the ship became very bad too, for none of the crew but the sail-maker, who was a good Christian man, paid any respect to the skipper, not even his officers. And he, poor old gentleman, unintentionally made matters harder for me by talking to me at the wheel, a mark of favouritism noted at once and savagely resented by my shipmates as a proof of my being a spy. It seemed a strange position to me that he aft and I forrard should both be so completely shut off from the sympathies and affections of our shipmates. Yet any breach in the unwritten but inexorable rules of sea etiquette, such as he did occasionally indulge in by talking to me in a friendly manner, was sure to culminate sooner or later in big trouble for both of us. Already the three officers were 'down' on me, not because of my work—for that, thank God, they could find no fault with—but for the skipper's sake.

The whole thing culminated at last, one Saturday afternoon, in the Indian Ocean. The weather suddenly became very threatening, and as we had our fair-weather suit of sails bent, the skipper judged it prudent to shift the topsails and foresail for the best ones we carried. He therefore gave orders for all hands to turn out at 1 P.M. for the purpose, which meant that the watch to which I belonged would not get their usual afternoon below. Now in many ships, especially American ships, the crew are never allowed to feel that they have any right to an afternoon watch below, but the general practice is to give the men the time, reserving the right to call on them in any case of necessity. Our watch, however, flatly refused to come on deck, with the sole exception of myself. Then the skipper called them aft and reasoned with them (how paltry and ridiculous this will sound to sailors of the old school!), but for all answer they gave him scurrilous abuse, while the officers stood by and said nothing. There was a great deal of talk, but in the end they went forrard again, leaving me to go on with the watch on deck.

I do not wish to do more than hint at the nature of the remarks made to me by my watch-mates, except to say that they comprised promises of hideous bodily injury worthy of the invention of Iroquois Indians, and that, in the result, without my saying one word or taking a single precaution, not a hand was lifted against me. It was an experience that did me a vast amount of good.

CHAPTER XIII

A STEADY SET-BACK

BEFORE leaving for ever the subject of this particular ship, I must gratefully record one incident that cheered me very much. It happened after the mutiny of which I spoke on the last page of the preceding chapter, and long after the skipper had given up in despair his well-meant endeavours to hold service for his crew's benefit. One lovely night I was sitting alone, as usual, on the forehatch, communing with my own heart in the solemn stillness of my surroundings, when one of my watchmates, a simple-minded, good-natured fellow enough if the other fellows would only have left him alone, came and flung himself down by my side. Without any preliminary but a startled glance all around to see if anyone was near, he said : ' Look 'ere, ole man, I sh'd like ter know sumfin 'bout this 'ere 'ligion o' yourn. I've heerd lots o' stuff talked by mishnaries an' parsons, but I couldn't never make nuthin' out of it. On'y I b'en watchin' yer fer a long time now, an' it fair licks me 'ow yer kin go on all this time with all hans a-chippin' at yer and yet ye don't seem a bit mis'bul. I sh'd a b'en fair loony long ago, jumped overboard or sumfin.'

To put the matter on the lowest ground, I was certainly much delighted at the chance of a little rational conversation on the one subject above all others that interested me, as well as proud that my conduct had met, in one instance at least, with the approval of a shipmate, however humble. So with a silent word for sanctified common sense, I began to talk. And he listened with almost painful intensity of earnestness until eight bells struck. In a few minutes we went below to turn in, but the moment we entered the door my auditor was greeted with a burst of blasphemous inquiries, which I would not, even if I dared, repeat. 'Yes, you're a —— lot of beauties, you are. There ain't the pluck o' one louse among th' ole lot of yer. Anybody'd think each of yer kep a privit berryin' groun' o' yer own, the way yer sling yer jaw, but ther' ain't one of yer 'at's dared ter lay a finger on this yer man ye've be'n a-threatenin' of all the passage. But I'm bettin' my bottom dollar 'at if the ship was a-goin' down you'd all be —— well a-howlin' ter

God Awlmighty to save yer dirty little rags o souls. W'y, y' ain't got 'arf a soul between th'ole gang. Garn, I've a seen better men et up be cockroaches afore now.'

I have only faintly indicated, for obvious reasons, the swear words with which this harangue was so forcibly punctuated, but it may be taken for granted that they were plentiful and pungent. Their effect, too, was instantaneous. The rage of the fellows was so violent that, for the first time that voyage, I really expected they would proceed to the last extremity. So I leaned over the side of my bunk (I slept immediately above my would-be champion), and said ' Don't say any more, there's a good fellow. You can't do any good, and it only makes matters worse for me. Wait ; you won't always be in a ship like this.' He looked up at me speechlessly for a moment, but made no further sign than to bury his face in his grimy pillow and take no more notice of anybody. And as I *never* took any notice of them, the tumult soon died away and quiet reigned.

We reached Calcutta without further incident, and I now reaped the benefit of the skipper's partiality by being allowed ashore whenever I wished to go This was nearly every evening and

all day Sunday, for here I rapidly found most
congenial quarters. But before going into the
matter of those pleasant times, I should like to
say that the mutineers were brought up before the
shipping master in Calcutta and fined two days' pay
for an action that might have jeopardised the ship
herself and struck at the very root of all authority,
besides being perfectly uncalled-for. Is it any
wonder that discipline is at a low ebb in the
British Mercantile Marine? Of course they all
returned on board again, firmly convinced that
they were at liberty to do as they pleased about
obeying orders, so long as they were willing to
forfeit a few shillings of pay.

And now I gladly acknowledge that, in spite
of the intense heat and generally trying climatic
conditions of Calcutta, I managed to pass a very
pleasant time. On Sundays I left the ship early
in the morning and did not return on board again
until about 10 P.M., dividing my time between the
comfortable room of Colonel Haig's Mission in
the Radha Bazaar, visiting the beautiful cathedral,
which was the coolest place I found in Calcutta,
and winding up the day with a hearty sing-song
on board the English Church Mission ship, where
everything possible was done to make such men

as would come feel welcome and honoured guests. It was a most delightful place. And to add to my pleasure, there was, at this time, a most marvellous outbreak of Christian enthusiasm among the British seamen visiting the port, chiefly due, I think, to the efforts of sundry American missionaries working at the Radha Bazaar Seamen's Rest. Large bodies of men might be seen returning on board their respective vessels at night, along the broad thoroughfares, singing with all their hearts, not Bacchanalian ballads, but sacred songs, sober, earnest, and full of devotional energy. The various keepers of the bazaar dens of all sorts of iniquity were in despair, for their trade was fast vanishing. Captains of ships met in dignified conclave to exchange wondering comment upon what most of them were pleased to call 'this psalm-singing fever.'

None of them, however, could deny that, whether they agreed or not with the spread of religion among sailors, the effect of the present extraordinary manifestation was entirely in their favour. The men worked better, gave no trouble by coming on board drunk, were in better health, and were undoubtedly happy. For my part, I am afraid that I was far too sanguine. In this

tremendous outpouring of the best gift of God
to men, I fancied I saw the first signs of a flood
of righteousness that should revolutionise the conditions of our Mercantile Marine, because I then
held precisely the same opinion as I do now—viz.
that the bettering of the sailors' conditions of life
and service can only be effectively obtained by the
personal elevation of his character. Laws without
end may be made, and only succeed in making
matters worse, because those who make them do
not, with the best possible intentions, understand
the subject, and under present conditions those
who should furnish them with the required information are content to curse and growl at their lot
while at sea, and when ashore devote all their time
and money to that which holds them down in the
dirt ; and the decent ones, despairing of doing
any good in their profession, seize an early opportunity of getting out of it. But a morally and
mentally uplifted *personnel* of the Merchant Service would be in a position to make their needs
known and get them supplied, to the great advantage of all concerned.

Let those sneer at Christian effort who will—
and God knows their name is Legion—there is no
more effective agent for the personal elevation of

man's body, as well as his soul, than this.   Other agencies lop off decayed branches or poisonous suckers ; Christianity strikes at the giant tap-root, and this alone can meet the urgent necessities of the case.

On the third Monday after our arrival the skipper sent for me, and told me that, as he had been forced to discharge the bo'sun for incompetency, he had been thinking of putting me in the vacant place.   But, fearing that with the same crew I should have a most unpleasant time of it, he had judged it kinder to try and get me a second mate's berth.   This he had now succeeded in doing, and if I were willing to forego the small amount of wages coming to me after my half-pay had been deducted, he would gladly give me my discharge.   Again I failed to see the justice of this ; indeed, it seemed to me more unjust than ever, because seamen's wages in Calcutta were just the same as the English, 3*l.* per month.   But I was met by the same alternative as before : I could either accept the terms offered or stay where I was. Of course this, under the circumstances, was no choice at all ; so I hesitated not a moment, and since I was obliged to accept, did so with as good a grace as possible.   He took me down at once to my new ship, a vessel of about the same size, but vastly superior in every detail, and in five minutes I had accepted the skipper's offer of 5*l*. 10*s*. a month, and a month's advance, which I at once despatched home to make amends for the half-pay which had now ceased.

Returning on board, I at once packed up, without being troubled at all by my shipmates. There was quite an affectionate little parting between my sturdy young champion—who had steadfastly set his face towards better things, in Calcutta—and myself. He naturally felt rather downcast at the prospect of the passage home, expecting with good reason that he would have a fiery trial of it. But I assured him that such an experience would do him no harm. By being compelled to rely entirely upon God, he would get a confidence unobtainable in any other way, just as one trusts a lifebuoy in reality only when obliged to hang on to it or drown. Thus we passed out of each other's lives and never saw or heard of one another again.

Full of gratification, I went on board my new ship, being received with much friendliness by the mate and third mate. She was loading jute for Dundee, and my first duty was to superintend the

stowing of the cargo.   The captain was seldom on
board, for, being half owner of the ship, he could
afford to please himself where he stayed while in
port.   Work went on with the regularity of a
well-oiled machine, and I could hardly congratu-
late myself sufficiently on having found so good
a ship.   When we got to sea it was just the
same, only now the skipper used to chat with me
familiarly, making me feel quite at home with him,
but also letting me see that he was a practical
pagan.   Once, indeed, he told me that he used
to conduct service on board, but finding it 'didn't
answer' he knocked it off.   I shuddered at the
idea.   Conduct divine service when the man's
whole life was a negation of divinity, and a selfish
pampering of every base appetite that suggested
itself to him !   But I said nothing.

Then came a black day when I suddenly
realised that, of all the unhappy times I had
spent at sea, this passage was going to be one of
the worst.   Between the skipper and the steward
there existed a strange fraternity, which had its
result in the latter behaving towards the officers
with a gross and insolent familiarity, such as I
have never before or since seen on board ship.
I had often wondered at the patient way in which

the mate, who was a middle-aged man and an excellent seaman, endured this treatment at the steward's hands, but put it down to a certain easy good-nature. To me the steward had said nothing at all but in a few civil monosyllables, until one afternoon he came to my cabin door and, without any preliminary, flung it wide open, saying ' Here, you, get me a cask o' beef when ye go on deck, 's quick 's the devil 'll let ye.' Aghast at this salutation, I could hardly speak for a moment—rage, surprise, shame, all struggled with me, impeding my speech. At last I said ' How dare you address me like that ? ' I had no time to say more, for he coolly said, 'Oh, you go t' hell. Just do as I told you, that's all.' Knowing full well that this kind of thing would be fatal to my position on board if allowed to go on, but, alas, not realising the futility of any attempt to alter it, I immediately went straight to the skipper and reported the steward for gross insolence and foul abuse. To my stupefaction, all he replied was, ' Look here, don't you get interfering with my steward, or it will be the worse for you. He's a dam sight better man than you are any day.' ' That may be true, sir,' I answered ; ' but at the same time I must remind you that you engaged me as third in command of this ship, and that during the six weeks that I have been on board you have had no fault to find with me. Why, then, do you now propose to subject me to the coarse domination of a domestic servant, knowing, as you must do, that I shall at the same time lose all power of command over my watch, down to the smallest boy?'

To this appeal he merely rejoined, 'You seem to have an infernal lot of back slack. Go away.' I went, down-hearted, for I could now most plainly see what a miserable time of it I was going to have. Fortunately, I did not know how bad it was going to be. Without the slightest wish to be commiserated or to represent my condition as worse than it was, I declare that every species of indignity that my skipper could devise he thenceforward put upon me. That I should have no privacy, he made the carpenter take my door off its hinges; that the men should rebel and curse me he would give me orders to do certain things while the crew were resting, as in the dog-watches or on Sundays, and then, when he could hear the row they were making, he would come on deck and ask me 'what the devil' I was doing, messing about like that. 'That'll do, men,' he would say in a commiserating voice to the men and with a sneering look at me. He deprived me of my rest until I could barely snatch three hours' sleep out of the twenty-four, and tried his best to goad me into some overt act of rebellion, in which, thank God, he did not succeed. But his treatment of me so affected the third mate, who had served his time in the ship, that he said, 'I thank God that it isn't me he's serving like this, for I should have been guilty of murder.'

And to crown all, after a passage of five months —nearly four months of incessant torture—this magnanimous gentleman did what in him lay to ruin my career by giving me a discharge marked 'G,' which is quite the equivalent of 'No good' in the case of an officer. Fortunately for me, I had already my mate's certificate, or I could not have obtained it, since it is indispensable to have a recommendation from your last skipper, and that I, of course, did not get. However, the voyage was over, I had done nothing to regret beyond coming in the ship at all, and a delightful welcome awaited me in our little back-room in Camden Town, where I was able, for a short time at any rate, to forget the miserable past.

But when I contrast the speed with which

those happy hours flew, with the leaden-footed days and weeks and months of that terrible passage home, I am compelled even now to sigh, and wonder why it is that pleasure is so short and pain is so long.

Very unwillingly, but with a certain sense of duty nearly forgotten, I return to that unhappy time just to note that through a great part of it I seemed to be utterly forsaken by God. No, not utterly forsaken—I don't believe I ever felt that quite—but left for a long time to 'dree my weird,' as the Scotch say. But I can well remember how I set my teeth, determined to endure doggedly to the end ; not hopefully looking forward—the time seemed too remote for that—but, as I have often done since when surrounded by troubles and unable to see a break in the clouds anywhere, just summoned up all the endurance I could find and gone on. It is a peculiar frame of mind, somewhat akin to hopelessness, and yet I cannot conceive of any man who has entirely lost hope living on. Both the mood and its effects, though often experienced by me, are a profound mystery to me still, but I feel sure that many besides myself have been similarly situated.

A certain fear comes upon me that the misery

of these later days of my sea life must seem painfully monotonous. Very gladly would I brighten them, for God knows that I was as susceptible to a stray gleam of sunshine as a sensitive plant; only, this being fact and not fiction, I am not able to do as I would in the matter. Yet, for the same reason that I was so sorely tried by untoward circumstances, I was always eager and ready to grasp the brightnesses of my life as they occasionally appeared, and to feel grateful to God for the mercies I always enjoyed. This, I think, is one of the most—well, call it by the commonplace word 'useful' things about the Gospel, that while it endows its recipients with a hope beyond all thought, a sure and certain hope for the future, it does at the same time so increase their sensitiveness and appreciation of all that is really joy-giving in this life, that no people on earth are really so happy as they, in proportion as they are, in very deed and in truth, followers of the Sorrowful Man.

Thus the few brief days I now spent at home (ah, what that word meant to me now!) were brimful of delight which not even the shadow of coming separation could dash from us. But as the small 'pay-day' dwindled away, and still my daily visits to the docks did not result in my getting a berth, I became so anxious that it was day by day more difficult for me to summon up a smile—only another proof, of course, that I was unable to learn the lesson of how to 'rest in the Lord' unless compelled to do so, which is a very different thing. However, the entire attitude of the mind of the child of God in the face of repeated manifestations of God's protecting care and solicitude for his best interests has been set forth so fully once for all in the story of Elijah that each individual experience is only a repetition of that sublime confidence when confronted by a veritable Himalaya of dreadful possibilities and dishonourable mistrust before molehills of trial, each phase ebbing and flowing in obedience to some mysteriously wayward influence within, and seems to be the portion of all, in every age, who have realised what God is to His people.

Once more I found it impossible to get a ship in London as officer. And, as before, I was driven at the last to ship before the mast as A.B. And now I felt that I had touched bottom almost in my profession, because the vessel I obtained was only a small Nova Scotian brigantine, bound to Cape Breton in the fall of the year, in ballast. I received a month's advance of 3*l.*, and sailed from the

Surrey Commercial Docks, finding, to my surprise, that I was far more comfortable than I had ever dreamed of being. For the vessel, though little more than three hundred tons burden and built of soft wood, was such a wonderfully sea-kindly craft, her skipper was so amicable, and her tiny crew so well fitted for their work, that the labour was immensely lightened by the pleasure that any seaman was bound to take in it. Besides, there was a great hope in my mind that things would surely mend now ; also the voyage would be short, and there would be, I expected, many chances of getting an officer's berth on the other side.

We were nearly a month on the passage, owing to baffling winds, but the vessel's behaviour was so good that it did not seem as long as that. Our only trouble was that we had shipped a cook in London who was so grotesquely incapable of doing anything in the cooking way, and so foully unclean besides, that we were compelled, in self-defence, to attend to the preparation of our own food.

Had the mate been allowed to deal with the pseudo-cook, I feel sure that murder would have been done ; but the skipper, though young and full

of vigour, was one of the most humane men I have
ever met, and he would not allow the poor impostor
to be maltreated.   Indeed, I have often seen the
fine fellow in the galley preparing some meal for
the cabin, while the cook hovered about outside,
looking wistfully at his commander's actions, but
never by any chance learning to do anything
correctly.   Many cooks have I seen, and at the
hands of many of them have I suffered, but never
have I come across anyone quite so bad as this
poor useless creature.

We duly arrived at Sydney (Cape Breton), and
after we had been at anchor about a week, the
news came that we were to proceed to Lingan, a
tiny port in Nova Scotia, to load soft coal for St.
John, New Brunswick.   Why, I did not understand,
since there were only three vessels in this quite
considerable coaling port, and an enormous supply
of coal awaiting shipment.   One of these vessels
had attracted the attention of everybody on board
when we entered the harbour, by her antiquated
and clumsy appearance.   She looked indeed as if
she was the result of some boat-builder's efforts to
build a sea-going ship, being just like an exaggerated wherry.   She was brig-rigged, her two masts
sticking up out of the curious hull like partly

broken broom-handles, and her jibboom pointing skyward at a most absurd angle. Her rigging was made out of the shabbiest entanglement of odds and ends I had ever seen pretending to fulfil the duties of a ship's upper gear, and the men, who stared listlessly over the side at us as we came in, were fully in keeping, a dirty, dispirited-looking handful of men. Had I met her in the Indian seas, I should have taken her for a 'country-wallah,' *i.e.* one of those funny old craft that, having survived their usefulness at home, have drifted into the hands of natives, who make a good deal of money out of them in the Indian coasting trade. It will presently be seen why I am thus particular in describing her.

The day for our departure arrived, the mate having informed us that we were to sail at 10 P.M. Shortly after dark he came forrard, and putting his head into the fo'csle, he called me. When I came out, he said in a mysterious whisper, 'Ye've got a mate's ticket, haven't yeu?' 'Yes,' I replied wonderingly. 'Well,' he went on, 'th' ole man sez that ef yeu like, yeu k'n clear out befo' we git under way. He ken't discharge ye 'thout a lot of trouble, 'n ye hain't got any dollars deu t' ye; so if yew'll say the word, my brother, who's 'longside naow with his boat, givin' me a look up, 'll give ye a shove ashore. Ef I wuz yeu, I'd jump at the chance, fur they's one ef not two ships in Sydney wantin' a mate, and they'll be all-fired glad t' git ye.' Need I say that I didn't hesitate a minute in accepting the offer, and bidding him give the skipper my most earnest thanks for his kindly thoughtfulness. And in three hours from thence I was being pulled shoreward with all my belongings. The mate's brother, after landing me on the beach and helping me ashore with my dunnage, said 'So long!' and shoved off for his home, leaving me there sitting on my bag, feeling as much alone as if I had been the sole survivor of a crew stranded on a desert island.

CHAPTER XIV

AN APPALLING VOYAGE

THERE was not a light in the little straggling town that I could see, and the night was very dark ; so for a while I sat still on my bag of clothes, trying to think out the situation. But do what I would, I could not suppress a miserable feeling of being deserted, like a lost child who blames its mother. This feeling was intensified by the melodious cries of my late shipmates as they got the pretty craft under way, and also by the damp chill of the winter night in that severe climate. At last, as a numbing sensation of cramp stole over me, I staggered to my feet, muttering 'Lord, help me, for I fear I'm in evil case now ;' and, leaving my bag where it was, groped my way up the bank of loose stones until I reached the street, if the long disconnected series of mean buildings could be dignified by such a name. Turning irresolutely from side to side, I saw a gleam of light through the crack of a door about a hundred yards away.

Without one thought of the impudence of my proceeding, I went straight towards it and tapped smartly with my knuckles against the door. A rough-looking man, in shirt and trousers only, barefooted and bareheaded, answered, and, with a sympathetic note in his voice, made me cordially welcome to such shelter as he had to give. There was already, he said, a drunken sailor of some sort lying on the floor, but I might take ' th' 'ould sofy.'

I thanked him heartily, as well I might, and hurried away to fetch my bag. When I returned he was waiting for me with a glass of rum, which I took gladly, for I felt chilled to the marrow. Then, bidding me good night, he retired into an inner room and left me in total darkness, with the stertorous breathing of my unknown companion in misfortune for a lullaby. It proved ineffective, for between the myriads of fleas which inhabited the couch, and the cold, I could not sleep at all. But I managed to while away the night somehow, and as soon as it was light enough to see I wandered down the street until I came to an ' hotel.' Here, after some vigorous knocking, I managed to gain admission, and upon telling my story I was cordially welcomed. Returning for my bag, I found my worthy host had not yet turned out, nor had the other lodger aroused, so I just shouldered my belongings and left.

As soon as working hours commenced I went a-hunting for the shipmaster of whom I had been told who wanted a mate, and very soon found him with a crony, sitting drinking brandy. As I was desperate, no false modesty restrained me from attacking him at once with the query, ' I hear you are in want of a mate, sir?' He looked at me with that peculiar air of judicial gravity affected by his class when liquor is just stirring their sluggish brains, and said 'Yes, I am. Are you a mate? Have you got a first mate's certificate?' By the precision and carefully clipped syllables of his speech, I knew him at once for a Welshman; by his bleared, furtive eyes and suffused face, I knew him for a drunkard; but these impressions registered themselves on my brain with the speed of light, and I replied courteously to his questions.

It appeared, from what he said, that he was not at all anxious to engage a mate just then—in fact, he would much rather not; but if I wanted a ship very badly, he didn't mind taking me on at once. By these careful lies he succeeded in getting me for a very low salary, for I was much afraid of

T

losing the chance, having found that there was no other vessel there that wanted a mate. No sooner had I agreed to go than we adjourned to a general store a few doors off, which, it appeared, was the shipping office, and there I signed the articles, which, for some strange reason, were already there. Then, turning to me, he said: 'Now look 'ere, Misser Bewlow' (he never got any nearer my simple name than that), 'I want you t' go on board and take charge. I am not very well, and shall go and lay down in my hotel a little while. You will find the second mate aboard, and he will introduce you to the ship. And if you want anything, just come ashore up to the hotel and see me about it.'

Promising to do his bidding after I had despatched my month's advance home, I left him, and in about an hour was down at the landing-place. There I found a melancholy little group of half a dozen men just dragging out of the water the dead body of a stalwart young seaman that had drifted on to the beach. Upon inquiry, I found that he had been one of my new ship's company, who had fallen overboard out of the boat the night before at sunset, as he was coming ashore to fetch one of his shipmates who was drunk. I could not help feeling that this was an inauspicious opening to my new venture, but when I got on board I found it was entirely appropriate. The second mate *was* on board, certainly ; but in a state of fury against the skipper, and firmly resolved never to do a stroke of work on board again. He told me a lurid yarn about the condition of things on board ; how they lived just from hand to mouth, buying a few pounds of stores here and there ; how they had been out from England nearly two years, during which time they had shipped five different mates ; and how the skipper had drunk every penny of freight earned by the ship, &c. &c. Between whiles the narrator relieved the tempest of his feelings by bursting into a torrent of Welsh, and when he had thus let off steam, as it were, he would go on more coherently until he got worked up again.

The condition of the vessel, on deck and in the cabin, was deplorable. I suppose it will already have been surmised that she was the quaint brig-rigged thing which had so excited our scornful laughter when coming into harbour, but the view we then obtained of her revealed very little of her true condition. My heart sank within me when I saw the filth everywhere and noticed the sullen looks of the five men forrard, doubly miserable now from the loss of their shipmate. However, she stood between me and starvation, not only for myself, but for another far dearer ; and with a short, almost fierce prayer for courage and ability to see the thing through, I began. It was almost hopeless from the outset to get any assistance from the second mate, who had fully made up his mind to take any risks in order to get clear of the ship ; but I kept on good terms with him, so that if he should alter his mind I might have the benefit of his services at once. I started the men at work to clean up a bit, at which there was a good deal of muttering that I could not afford to take any notice of. Indeed, the only pleasant face that appeared on board was owned by a chubby lad, the nephew of the skipper, who, fearfully and wonderfully grubby, was performing, after a weird fashion, the double offices of cook and steward.

In two days the old tub began to look a little more as a ship that is still sea-going should look, and I was becoming more contented. But meanwhile a sorrowful thing occurred which I feel I must record, although I am afraid it will be fiercely disputed by some people. The poor fellow who was drowned was a native of Clonakilty, co. Cork, and a most devout Catholic. He had also won the sincere regard of his shipmates by his good life, as well as genial, kindly behaviour. So that when the time came for him to be buried they all asked to go ashore to attend his funeral. Therefore, leaving the second mate and boy on board, we all went up to the little churchyard, where we found a group of bewildered men surrounding the rough coffin. They did not know what to do, because the parish priest had refused to perform the burial service. I make no comment; I repeat none of the remarks made by these indignant Catholics; I merely record the fact that the body was silently lowered into the grave, and one of the rough labourers knelt down on the newly turned soil and commended the poor soul to God. I said nothing, because personally I feel that, although it is undoubtedly right and becoming to put our dead away from us with solemnity and decorum, whatever we do or say affects not the piece of clay that was our friend at all. But I know that multitudes of dear people think otherwise, and would be sorely wounded at such a graveside scene as this.

We all returned on board very quietly and did not resume work that day. The next morning I went ashore at nine and sought my commanding officer. Being told to go up to his room, I found him in bed with a half-emptied bottle of brandy by his side, in a maudlin state of drunkenness. He was able, however, to give me instructions not to trouble him any more than I could help, as he was not at all well, to tell me the name of the agent for loading the ship, and to order me to use my best endeavours to get the coal in and the ship ready for sea ; also, to report progress to him now and then. I left his presence disgusted, yet consoled by the reflection that he was having his debauch on shore, where he was out of the way. Then I went to a surgeon and had an operation performed for a whitlow on my left thumb, that left me one-armed for over two months and has practically crippled the digit for life. Thenceforward, left to my own resources, getting no sleep for the pain of my thumb until utterly exhausted, and always scheming some way of utilising the few bits of rotten gear on board, to make things at least a little shipshape, I had no time to be miserable. In fact, I believe that the experience was distinctly salutary. Its very sordidness and hopelessness and loneliness compelled me to seek for the comfort I stood so much in need of, where alone it could be found.

The crew, if listless and careless, were not hostile, and, so long as I was content to let them go at their own pace, evidently did not mean to give me any trouble. The second mate loafed about all day trying my patience sorely, but I had nothing to gain by endeavouring fruitlessly to force him to his duty against his will, so I bore with him. And in due time the cargo was on board, the sails bent, the vessel shifted out into the bay from the coal tips, and everything ready for sea. Then I visited the skipper and informed him of the fact, but he had in nowise exhausted the delights of his prolonged carouse, and for another twenty days we remained there, idly swinging at our anchor. Every morning I saw him, every morning he made excuses for not going to sea, generally that he was ill ; until at last the consignee of the cargo in St. John having worried the agent into desperation, that gentleman came on board, and, after ascertaining from me how matters really stood, went to the skipper's lodgings and threatened to give me orders to take the ship to sea without him unless he instantly returned to his duty. This menace of the agent's, although I do not think he would have dared to carry it out without instructions from the owner, was effectual. The old man came on board two hours after in a small tug, and, having given me orders to get under way, retired to his cabin in company with a large wicker-covered jar of spirits. From thence he did not again emerge until we reached St. John three weeks after.

Want of space prevents me from giving more than the merest outline of that passage. Moreover, I am fully convinced of my utter inability to do justice to its details. Only a sailor could realise what it meant to me to be alone in charge of an unhandy old brig, deep-loaded with coal, on one of the most dangerous coasts in the world, in the middle of November, with only one hand to use, and no one to relieve me in whom I could place confidence; for the second mate, baulked of his wish to leave in Sydney, refused to keep a watch. And on the first occasion of taking sights for longitude, I found the chronometer to be hopelessly wrong. This was partly my own fault, for though I had carefully attended to the winding of the instrument ever since I had been on board I had not tested its accuracy, as prudence should have suggested. When I discovered that it was useless, I felt for a moment as if all was lost, but soon recovered, and from that time I worked my way cautiously south by the aid of the deep-sea lead and the fishing schooners. But if ever a man was 'instant in prayer,' I was. I grew confident that we should make out all right, even though I knew it would be little short of miraculous if, with such a 'clumbungie,' we successfully manœuvred through the tremendous tide races and conflicting currents from Cape Sable to the Grand Manan, where I hoped to get a pilot.

An elderly seaman of great experience used to keep a look-out for me while I snatched uneasy periods of sleep, and one night, amidst a sleet storm of great violence, I awoke just in time to see, through a momentary break, the beam from Cape Roseway Lighthouse shining overhead. Not until we had clawed off on the other tack and lost sight of the light astern did I fully realise how narrow had been our escape. Although the night was bitterly cold I was drenched with sweat, induced, I supposed, by the violent nerve strain. But when we came to the place I dreaded most of all, the Bay of Fundy, the weather fined and kept beautifully clear until, with the pilot on board, I was able to take the first solid four hours' sleep I had enjoyed for three apparently interminable weeks.

The skipper went ashore as soon as we reached
the pier next day, although he had previously been
too unwell to leave his cabin since we left Sydney :
that is, he had been too busily engaged in empty-
ing his brandy jar and suffering the penalty for
so doing. But he was a truly marvellous man.
In spite of his excesses, his close confinement, and
lack of food, he did not look the wreck that one
would have expected him to be. However, ashore
he went, muttering his formula, ' I'm not very well.
Think I sh'll stay ashore to-night.' Whether he
had a dim idea of catching me at some nefarious
practices or not, I do not know ; but he returned
that night, and, utterly ignoring the lighted gang-
way I had caused to be rigged from the quay to
the main rigging, walked deliberately over the edge
of the wharf and fell a matter of fifty feet into the
mud, the tide being out. In his fall he passed
between the vessel's side and the piles of the
wharf ; he struck in the only position in which it
was possible for him to do so and not be killed—
feet foremost—and when, in response to his piteous
cry of ' Misser Bewlow, Misser Bewlow, for Gaw's
sake safe my lyve !' we rescued him, he was no
whit the worse, with the exception of a few bruises,
for his awful fall ; indeed, he was still drunk.

Next morning he was assisted to a carriage and taken to an hotel, where he remained during the whole of our stay in St. John. I used to visit him occasionally, and always found him the worse for liquor.

All this time I had steadfastly refused to touch anything stronger than tea or coffee, nor would I ever take any money from him, although he was continually proffering it; for I wanted all my pay when I got home, oh! so badly. There was another way open to me to make money, of which I refused to avail myself, although, as the event proved, I might have done so without wronging anybody but myself—which, I take it, is the best argument against practices of the kind to which mates of sailing ships were, in my day, peculiarly liable. The old vessel had an enormous quantity of 'junk'—old rope and canvas—on board, because in Santos she had been fitted with wire rigging, and the skipper, instead of bargaining to exchange the old gang of rope-rigging for it, had paid cash, thereby securing an ample cash commission for himself. Now by some means it became known ashore in St. John that all this old junk was aboard of us, and I was continually being pestered by 'longshoremen' to sell it to them or to recommend my skipper to sell it to them. For this latter service-one man offered me as much as twenty-five dollars—that is, he was willing to give a hundred dollars for the junk, of which I might retain twenty-five for myself. Others offered less sums, and I refused to have anything to do with them at all. But somehow the hundred-dollar man found the skipper out and succeeded in inducing him to sell the junk for seventy-five dollars, besides so ingratiating himself with the poor sot that he was engaged as stevedore, to go with us to our port of loading and stow the vessel's cargo.

When this worthy came, armed with the skipper's order to cart away the junk, he was exceedingly sarcastic at my honesty, which he characterised in familiar but unquotable language. And I admit that, from an outsider's point of view, it was hard to see where the benefit to anybody but the purchaser came in.

I was unable to get away from my ship at all, except for a brief space on Sunday mornings, as there was no other officer on board, the second mate having succeeded in getting his discharge and pay, and no other having been engaged ; and, as no one came to see me, I was still quite alone, as far as human companionship was concerned.

On Sunday mornings I used to go to a Church of England near by for the sweet sense of rest and aloofness from the world that it gave, although the way that the service was gabbled over and the utter paltriness of the preaching used to make me sick at heart. No one ever spoke to me. Why should they? I don't suppose I looked very companionable, for although I was so young I had a preoccupied, reserved, and elderly appearance—rather repellent, I do not doubt.

After a stay of three weeks the skipper arrived one day with his crony, the 'tagarene' man, and a large supply of brandy. He informed me with great dignity that we were to load lumber, deal planks, at a little port called Parrsboro', in the basin of Minas, near the place immortalised by Longfellow in 'Evangeline.' Of course we were to tow over there—over a hundred miles, I think. There never was such a man for accumulating towage expenses. I was not sorry, for it relieved me of a great deal of worry and hard work. We started that afternoon, and were no sooner clear of Partridge Island than the skipper and his chum, being both too drunk to stand, retired below, and I saw them no more during the passage. The night passed entirely without incident, but upon arriving in the river next day and taking up a local pilot, I could get no information from the skipper where we were to lie ; and as no harbour-master appeared, we were fain to tie up at the first wharf that we reached. Then the pilot and I trudged through the snow for a couple of miles to the village, it being now dark, where I managed to find the consignee, who told me what wharf to come to, but was very curious about the indisposition of the skipper.

Thank heaven, my miserable position was soon to be altered. It had been bad enough before but now it had become intolerable. This drunken blackguard of a stevedore, when he was not carousing with the skipper ashore in an hotel to which they had both departed the day following our arrival, was directing a couple of men to fling the lumber about the hold. Stowage there was none. When I remonstrated with this shameful proceeding, for by it the vessel was rendered unseaworthy (and she had to face a North Atlantic winter passage), he jeeringly referred me to the skipper, who, he said, had told him he was not to be interfered with. I went to the skipper and tried to make him understand what was being done, but all that I could get out of him was that

'Chimmy' was a good man, who knew his business, and that I had better let him alone. That broke down the high barrier of patient endurance I had so carefully erected, and I told him, with some heat I am afraid, that under such conditions I would not go in the ship. At which he laughed, and ordered me to go on board.

Next day he came down to visit the ship. We were all at dinner, when we heard a tremendous crash, and, rushing on deck, we found that he had in some mysterious way fallen between the ship and the wharf, breaking the ice, which was several inches in thickness. We dragged him out, unhurt except for a few bruises and scratches. Without even changing his clothes, only taking a blanket to wrap round him, he returned to his hotel and stayed there. I afterwards heard that a few days previous he had gone for a sleigh ride with his crony and had been pitched head foremost over a steep bank into a great snowdrift, where he was dug out with enormous difficulty, but entirely unhurt, and not even sobered.

The day arrived when the ship was loaded—I cannot say she was ready for sea, for it is impossible to conceive of a ship more unfit to face even the simplest navigation than she was. She had a

deckload of deals, rising four feet above the rails—
that is, about eight feet in height—and was so
'crank' or topheavy that she would scarcely stand
upright at the wharf.   Her sails were like muslin
for thinness, besides being clouted, or patched,
until they looked like a nigger field-hand's breeches.
The men were afraid to put their weight on a rope
for fear of bringing something tumbling about their
ears.   And she was almost bare of provisions.   So
I sat down and wrote a letter to the owner, briefly
setting forth the state of affairs, telling him that I
was firmly convinced that it was the skipper's
intention to cast the ship away, and that, under all
the circumstances, I did not feel justified in going
to sea in such a vessel.

Then I went up to the hotel, where, at ten in
the morning, I found the skipper and 'Chimmy'
in the same bed, looking as frowsy and besotted
and animalised as any two human beings I ever
saw, and I have seen some gorgeous specimens.
Only Zola could do justice to the details of that
chamber, and then the reading would not be to
our taste.   Without any preface I said, 'Captain,
I want my discharge.'   This roused him, and after
its import had soaked into his bemused mind, he
answered as shortly, 'You can't have it.'   I am

not going to detail the conversation that followed, for even the recalling of the scene is most unpleasant for me, and I am afraid it would be doubly so for my readers. In the event, I left him and returned on board, removing my effects to an hotel, whose proprietor, in full knowledge of the conditions, had promised to receive me. I then consulted a lawyer, premising that I was penniless and that he could only be paid in the event of my succeeding. He advised me to have the skipper arrested on a writ of Capias, saying that it would bring matters to a head. I followed his advice; the skipper was arrested just as he was going on board, and had a tug alongside to tow the vessel to St. John, where I suppose he intended to ship another unfortunate mate.

But, as I might have expected had I been more experienced in such matters, I was hopelessly beaten. To my intense amazement, the strongest point upon which I had relied—the danger resulting to the ship's company from the skipper's habitual drunkenness —failed completely. He swore that he was temperate, and that he had never been intoxicated since he had commanded the ship. He was far from sober at the time of making this statement, by the way; but the court, such as it was, believed him

U

and as my counsel had called no witnesses, this monstrous lie passed. In vain I pleaded the unseaworthiness of the ship, the fact of my having no officer to relieve me; the only alternatives presented me were to sail in her or lose my wages. But, as I said to the lawyer, although I sorely needed that 12*l*., I did not feel like risking so much to obtain it. So the brig was towed away, and, to cut my story short, the skipper spent a fortnight in St. John drinking, then shipped another mate and sailed, losing the vessel (and three men's lives) before he had gone a hundred miles, which was what I was firmly convinced he meant trying to do.

My position was now a serious one. I had no money, and although my hotel bills only amounted to three dollars a week, they were mounting up. Navigation was fast becoming impossible for ice, for winter was now almost at its height. I felt like a rat in a trap. But I have always found that the apparently hopeless cases of difficulty that have confronted me have disappeared miraculously at the touch of God's hand or ever I came upon them. This was to be no exception to the good rule. Meanwhile I found some congenial society among the Episcopalians, and became, for the time, a member of their choir. None of them knew, however, to what straits I was reduced; and even had they known, I fear the circumstance of a man being compelled to get into debt through enforced idleness during the winter was far too common to excite any wonder.

Relief came at last. I had been about three weeks ashore, when a ragged-looking ruffian one morning accosted me with 'Say, 'r yeu th' duck 'at's lookin' for a ship? Mate ain't ye?' I gazed at him wonderingly, but I had learned that in Nova Scotia clothes do not make the man, so I answered him carefully. Whereupon he told me that he had built a schooner of twenty-four tons, which he had loaded with potatoes grown on his own farm, and he was now anxious to take her out to the West Indies to sell her and her cargo if possible. But he wanted a navigator, and was willing to pay twenty-five dollars a month for one. Would I come? Indeed I would, if he would only give me a month's advance. He agreed, although it is a mystery to me how he raised the money; for he was poor, with a poverty that was pathetic— so poor that he could not buy reasonable food for the passage. He managed to raise enough for my advance though, on paper. Here again was a difficulty. I wanted sadly to send ten dollars home, but could find no one to let me have cash for my note. I could buy things with it, anything the stores contained ; but no dollars were forthcoming, and at last I was driven to asking the skipper to take his note back and give me fifteen dollars advance, which was all I needed to pay my score and make my few purchases. This he did with alacrity. I wound up my affairs, came on board the tiny craft, and squeezed myself into the little square foul-smelling den of a cabin with my belongings. I found that a small boy of twelve, the skipper's son, and a half-witted lad of fifteen were to accompany us, both looking as dirty and woebegone as possible. And twenty-four hours after meeting with my rough-looking commander we were bowling down the Basin of Minas, bound for summer.

CHAPTER XV

AND LAST

DURING my stay in Parrsboro' I had found, to my amazement, that I was far better able to endure the intense cold than the natives, who used to work muffled up to the eyes in all sorts of strange woolly garments, and with double mitts on their hands, while I was bare-handed and in shirt-sleeves. They told me that this was usually the case with new-comers in their first winter, but that if I stayed there a year I should find myself just as susceptible as they were. For the present, however, this ability to bear cold stood me in good stead, for when we were about forty miles from Parrsboro' the weather became terrible in its severity. 'Frost smoke' arose from the sea, creating an environment as much colder and more penetrating than ordinary low-temperature clear weather, as a snow-and-salt mixture is colder than ice water. Every little spray coming over froze where it touched, and every lurch of the vessel brought down a mass of glittering ice from above. We groped our way into Musquash Harbour and shipped a stock of wood and water, my mind filled with an unreasoning peevish anger against such miserable conditions of labour.

Leaving there the next day, we moved cautiously south, anchoring behind Bryer Island and in Yarmouth on successive days because we had got so frozen up we could not work the vessel. Unhappily, I now realised that my employer was a man of the worst class, brutal in his behaviour, blasphemous in his talk, and unutterably filthy in his habits. To be shut up with him and those two poor lads for what looked like being a month was so serious a prospect that I refused to consider it. We spent Christmas Day anchored at the entrance to Yarmouth Harbour, the weather being much too severe for us to venture out—so bad, in fact, that even in our tiny den, the floor-space of which was half filled by the stove, we could hardly keep from freezing, although the big boy was kept constantly employed thrusting blocks of birchwood into the fire.

On the fifth day after leaving Parrsboro' we reached a small anchorage at the back of Cape

Sable Island ; only just in time, for a tremendous gale commenced outside before we had got the sails furled. Here we lay for a week, until the vessel looked more like a tiny iceberg than aught else, our only food potatoes with a smack of salt herring about them. We had but a 'kit' (about twenty-five pounds) of these fish, and it was necessary to be economical with them, as our keg of beef had become putrid. We had a barrel of flour, with which the big boy made something like bread, salting it with his tears under the continued and shameful brutality of the skipper. For drink we had a decoction of burnt bread, neither tea nor coffee being included in our store list. But, after all, these were minor evils, not to be considered under the far graver conditions in which we were existing.

At last we managed to get ashore and enjoy a day's chopping among the young birches to re-plenish our stock of firewood, exercise which was delightful after the wretched cramped-up life we had been leading. And finally we cut down a spreading young spruce tree, leaving all its branches intact. This, with a vast amount of labour, we managed to get on board and secure across the main deck, which it completely filled

Then, the wind veering favourably, we broke the ice off our upper gear and put to sea.

It was the skipper's first watch on deck that night (we took four hours each, as neither of the boys were of any use to us), and when he called me at midnight I awoke with a sense of relief and gratitude unspeakable. For the bitter bleak edge of the cruel winter we had exchanged the mild balmy atmosphere of the Gulf Stream. Already the ice and snow had almost disappeared, the ropes felt soft, the sails flapped instead of snapping and crackling like wood. My misery fell from me like a shroud, and I longed to sing. Ah, how thankful I was! This blessed relief had but just time to revive us, when bad weather set in. A heavy gale arose, blowing right across the set of the Gulf Stream, and raising a mighty succession of such dangerous waves as cannot be excelled anywhere in the world. So we played our last card : we shackled our cable to the bole of our spruce tree and hove it overboard. It acted as well as any sea-anchor ever made, keeping the poor little vessel's head up to the sea. And thus, with every stitch of canvas as secure as we could make it, we lay for seventy-two hours, a mere chip in that howling ocean. Nine watches of four hours each I stood by the useless wheel, watching the never-ending succession of roaring green mountains rushing towards us, and acutely conscious that each one was probably bearing us the stroke of grace. They were solemn hours to me, of which I cannot speak; but with deepest gratitude I record that whenever the skipper relieved me I went to my narrow bunk and immediately slept like a babe on its mother's bosom.

It was a fascinating, if a terrible experience, to stand and watch the oncoming wave soar higher and higher until, in thundering triumph, it was upon us and sweeping us away to leeward, as if we were only a feather; then the swift descent into the great hissing hollow between the wave just past and the wave just coming, while their foam-curdled surfaces in unnatural smoothness seemed to be sinking us to the ocean's bed. This ascent and descent, performed every minute or so during the whole of those three days, never lost its potentialities of terror; although, thanks to our novel sea-anchor, we rode gallantly. Only in the last burst of the gale the sea that I appeared to have been waiting for so long suddenly arrived. It caught the poor little craft in its full embrace, and what happened after is a blank for I was clinging for life to the wheel, and wondering how much longer I could hold my breath under water. And when I breathed again and could see, I found that she had suffered no damage. Not only so, but the weather had broken ; and as our tree-stem had been chafed right through, we made sail such as she would bear and edged away south.

With the coming of fine weather the skipper became quite jovial and confidential. He favoured me with full details of his plans for the future. He wasn't going back again, not he. His old woman and her litter might go to the devil, he'd done enough for 'em. No ; he would get rid of the boy somehow, and then he would make a bee-line for New York with the proceeds of the sale of his vessel, and set up a brothel—that was the best-paying game. And so on and so on for an hour at a time, while I stood at the wheel, sick at heart but unable to escape.

We had no more bad weather, and at fairly good speed we gradually lessened our latitude until we were far enough south, and, having no chronometer, began cautiously to steal west. We only met one vessel, strange to say, and that was when we were near enough for the longitude she

gave us to last us as a departure point until we
got safely into port.   And no sooner was the
anchor down and the sails fast than I hailed a
canoe, put my dunnage into it, and hastened
ashore.   For although I have not dared to enlarge
upon the matter, partly from dwindling space and
partly because I would not like it thought that I
was degenerating into a querulous grumbler, I had
really suffered a great deal on board that little
vessel from my compulsory association with that
man.   Physically filthy, repulsively blasphemous,
and outrageously cruel—he gave the poor half-
witted cook a kick in the mouth one day that
disfigured him for life and broke several of his
teeth—to be shut up with an animal like that in
so small a space for a month was as severe a trial
as I wish to undergo.

Whether he thought that it was unwise to
allow me to go to the shipping master alone or
not, I do not know ; but he followed me ashore
instantly and paid me the small amount I had
due, giving me my discharge in due form before
the shipping master.   I said as little to him as I
could, being only anxious to see his back ; and
finding me thus uncompanionable, he departed and
I saw him no more.   The shipping master very

courteously asked me what I proposed to do. I explained my position to him, and he then advised me to get away from St. John at once as there was practically no shipping there at any time that would suit me. He gave me an introduction to the skipper of a smart-looking schooner in the harbour, with the queerest name I ever heard, 'The Migumooweesoo,' who, he said, would gladly give me a passage to Barbadoes, and was leaving next day. There he was sure I should soon get a chance.

Of course I hastened on board at once, finding the skipper, a splendid young specimen of manhood, almost at death's door with dysentery. His crew were all negroes, kindly willing fellows enough, but not able to do for him what was needed, or keep him company ; consequently his delight at my advent was pathetic to see. He would hardly allow me to go ashore and fetch my few belongings, in case I should alter my mind and not come ; and I had no sooner returned than he gave his mate orders to get under way with all speed, as we had twenty horses on board and the question of their food was rather a serious one.

We made a very long passage of ten days, during which we were compelled to put into Prince Rupert, Dominica, for sugar-cane tops for the horses to eat ; but I was thoroughly happy. My small knowledge of common-sense medical treatment succeeded in pulling poor Brown out of the very jaws of death, while my company was to him, he said, more precious than he could ever have imagined such a thing could be. So that when we arrived in Barbadoes I had that satisfactory sense of being of some use—that is one of the sweetest feelings, I think, one can have in this world.

He would, however, hear nothing about Christ. When I first broached the subject he was terribly alarmed, and asked me most anxiously if I thought he was dying. The earnestness of my disclaimer reassured him, but he begged me not to mention the matter to him again unless I really thought he was going to die. He said that was all the use of religion that he knew of, to cheer people up when they were going 'off the hooks.' And when he got better he said such things about Christianity and Christians generally, that in my turn I begged him to let the matter drop.

I parted from him with a good deal of regret, for he was a thoroughly manly fellow ; only his moral nature had been warped from his youth up by vicious surroundings. And after hearing some of his stories of the relations between whites and coloured people of the island, I could well understand how, if there was any truth in them, he had come to look upon religion as the merest farce. But as that was a matter of hearsay only, and is besides somewhat out of my province, I must pass on.

Only a matter of ten days (though they were long days, I admit) passed in Bridgetown before I was one morning informed at the shipping office that there was a large barquentine in the harbour needing a chief mate. Without a moment's delay I hurried on board, finding her a truly splendid yacht-like craft and one that it would be a delight to command. I was received by the second mate, really the boatswain, for he was a man unable to read. He was a very genial fellow though, and looked every inch a sailor-man. That, however, I should have judged from the beautiful appearance of the ship. Glad, I suppose, to have some-one to talk to, he told me one of the most pathetic stories of the sea it has ever been my lot to hear. It appeared that they had but just come from Port Natal. On their departure they had been com-manded by a man of whom the rough boatswain spoke with bated breath as if he were no ordinary mortal. He was of huge stature, yet gentle as a child, a thorough seaman and navigator, and withal a simple-minded, great-hearted Christian. With him were his wife and two little ones, and to see him with those hostages to fortune was to wonder how one human heart could hold so much love. After a most perilous passage round the Cape, another little son was born to him away in the middle of the South Atlantic. But before he had nursed his precious helpmate quite back to strength again, he himself was stricken down by some terrible disease, about which neither the mate (now captain) nor his wife knew anything; and, after battling with it manfully for five or six days, he suddenly lost the desire of more life and quietly drifted homewards in the arms of his heart-broken helpmate. Four days later the vessel arrived in Barbadoes, where the hapless widow and her orphan children were transferred to the mail steamer and sent home.

By the time the second mate had finished his recital the skipper had arrived, and in the course of a few minutes we had arranged terms &c. The vessel was bound to the coast ports of the Gulf of Mexico for mahogany, whither I had sailed so many years before on my first voyage; and as the only reason she had for calling at Barbadoes at all was to get orders where to proceed, we sailed the next day. I felt very pleased indeed. The skipper, just promoted by circumstances, was cheerful and companionable and sober; the second mate, although to my mind a little too chummy with the skipper, was a good fellow enough; the crew were sturdy and willing sailor-men; and so the ship, taken all round, was as comfortable as she could well be. Too comfortable, I am afraid, for me; for I said not a word about my profession of Christianity when I first came on board, and ever afterwards I found it impossible. Sailing under false colours is always a risky as well as a dishonest proceeding, and in this instance especially it did me, spiritually, an immense amount of harm.

Not that I ever felt any desire to contract myself out of the Lord's requirements; but somehow the miserable fallacy was wrapping itself about my heart that the Master's service was bringing me always into trouble. I felt, as I know so many have felt, that while the service of God in the world was a glorious thing to die for, it was not so glorious a thing to live for. It meant a world full of enemies, misunderstandings and impositions; not, perhaps, so painful as the short sharp agony of the stake and the torture-chamber, but the long drawn-out suffering of continual enmity and separation from one's kind. And the subtle suggestion was constantly being made to me, not from any tangible person, 'What is the use of thus cutting yourself off from your kind like this? What good does it do? Even those good people ashore who preach at you and write books to you, telling you what sort of life you should lead, have no idea at all of your condition. They have home and wife and family and friends always at their hand. They lie warmly and securely, they eat pleasantly and regularly, and all the amenities of social life are theirs for the taking. God does not expect, then, from you that you should lead a life of martyrdom which can have no possible good result. He wants you, as well as those even-tempered teachers ashore, to have a few of the pleasantnesses of life.' And so on. The fallacies underlying all these thoughts were dimly apparent, but only dimly, and gradually the conviction forced itself upon me that I had been trying to be righteous overmuch and doing harm instead of good.

Had I only then met with someone who would have persecuted me, scoffed at my Master and Friend, and done despite to the Holy One I loved with all my heart, it would have been good for me, I think. But no ; I was allowed to drift a certain distance—not too far—and to wet my pillow at night with tears of repentance because I was not living up to the high standard I believed to be required of me by my loving Father. Ah me ! how little, after all the painful teaching I had endured, did I yet know of Him !

Nothing of any notable interest took place upon our passage down to Tonala. The days glided by most smoothly ; the work went on without a hitch. But on our arrival within the bar of Tonala River there was a change. The skipper and the second mate, inseparable now, took to making long excursions ashore, leaving me to carry on the work. And after a day's ramble, or a picnic, they would come on board, having invited their friends from the other vessels, and expect me to join them in an evening's carouse. This I could not do, for two reasons. One was that I had no taste or inclination for such affairs—that had all been taken from me long ago ; the other was that I felt my position very keenly as the first officer, being thus placed with regard to the second. For this is not merely a matter of wounded *amour popre* ; it is an essential part of discipline, by the maintenance of which alone is the due carrying out of ship duties possible. The crew are quick to note the smallest slight put upon an officer. If they like him they resent it ; if they dislike him they use it as a most efficient excuse for showing the dislike which he is powerless to resent. I merely mention this lest it should be thought that the notice taken of what may be considered amongst people in whose lives the maintenance of discipline has no part, is evidence of thinness of skin or morbid readiness to take offence.

However, I was determined to give no handle to my commander for a quarrel ; so, resolutely ignoring what was going on, I attended to my work, tallying in the cargo of mahogany logs ; and when cargo was delayed, keeping the vessel in trim and scouring the creeks for stranded waifs in the shape of log-ends that had broken adrift and were ownerless. These were split up into dunnage wood and utilised for ' broken stowage,' *i.e.* filling up interstices left in the hold by the ungainly masses of timber refusing to accommodate themselves to the curves of the ship. I got very little chance to go ashore, and what little I did get I seldom availed myself of ; for the place was utterly devilish. There was not even the faint

semblance of religion usually found in South
American coast towns, for the wild outlaws who
peopled the place would not tolerate a priest
among them, and used to recount with glee the
treatment meted out to a venturesome monk who
did dare to come and attempt to pursue his minis-
trations among them. They stripped him and set
him in the stocks beneath the burning sun for the
space of a whole day. When released, more dead
than alive, he was driven on board of a schooner
departing for Goatzocoalcos, and warned emphatically that on his next appearance there he would
be converted into dogs' meat.

It is surely needless for me to say that I was
glad when sailing day arrived. The last few days
of our stay were passed outside the bar, which did
not permit of us passing it fully laden, and the strain
upon me of getting those few remaining dozens of
logs on board without damage to the ship or my
men was considerable; so that I gave a great
sigh of relief when the last log swung inboard
and we ran up our 'full ship' flag. From that hour
I began to look across the wide sea homeward.

Now, while the skipper did not in the least
attempt to interfere with me in my working up the
ship's position from astronomical observations, and

allowed me the fullest access to the excellent pair of chronometers we carried, he never allowed me to compare my positions with his. He just looked at them and nodded, or muttered something, according to his mood, but his work I never saw. And I confess that I had a very strong feeling of nervousness about that great reef whereon I had been wrecked in my boyhood. So it was only natural that as we neared its neighbourhood, by my reckoning, I kept an extra vigilant outlook. And one night when the smart craft was flying along, with a quartering wind, under all canvas, at the rate of eleven knots an hour, I was called at midnight by the second mate as usual. But coming on deck my nostrils at once detected the strong 'reef-smell,' and although I had just risen from a sleep like that of the dead, I started aloft. Not a moment too soon. I had no sooner reached the foretopsail yard than I saw stretched out ahead that awful fringing wreath of snowy breakers, marking the presence of a coral reef. For a moment I could hardly find my voice. Then moistening my lips, I shouted 'Lee forebrace, below there ; keep her as high as she'll lie!' Up she swung into the wind, staggering like a stricken thing under the now tremendous pressure of canvas ; and as I saw that she pointed clear of the weather corner of that death-trap, I said quietly up there in the night, 'Thank God! thank God!'

Slipping downwards to the deck, I called the skipper, who was, as may be supposed, dreadfully alarmed. He went aloft immediately, and did not come down again until we at last swung clear of that terrible place and were once more able to resume our homeward course.

Thenceforward we had no more trouble. After a fairly good passage we entered Falmouth Harbour, whither we were bound for orders, and after a couple of days' stay, departed for Rotterdam, where the crew were discharged and only the skipper and myself remained behind. And here I had another experience similar to that quoted by me in St. John, N.B. As soon as the nature of our cargo became known, we were boarded by quite a crowd of nondescript fellows, mostly Jews, whose one object seemed to be the purchase of our dunnage wood. One of these men thrust a 5*l.* note into my hand, and upon my inquiring what his generosity meant, told me that it was because he had taken a great liking for me. He was, it was true, going to bid for the mahogany dunnage wood, but he did not wish me to bias the skipper in his favour at all.

Of course not; only he begged me to accept his little mark of regard. Well, the whole thing seemed so fishy that I refused, much to his astonishment and chagrin. He went away, and I saw no more of him until next day, when he came up to me, and smiling sarcastically, said, ' Vell, Meesder Mate, I haf puy de vood. Unt I tondt gif more for him dan I expecdt to. Now eef yu haf dake dat vife poundts yu vill be gladt unt I vill be sorry. But yu are so [English adjective] vool as not to dake him, zo I am gladt, unt yu ben sorry, hein! Pelief me, Meesder Mate, yu ben von [English adjective again] jackass.'

I turned away, having nothing to say; but when, a few days after, I found that my share of the proceeds of the wood, to which I was honestly and rightfully entitled, had been divided by the skipper between himself and the second mate, I was inclined to believe that my Hebrew critic was really not so wrong after all. And when the cargo was all out, the skipper informed me that, although he had no fault to find with me, his brother, who was a mate, was out of a ship, 'and of course you know a man must look after his own family.' So I departed homeward, glad to escape for a few days' domestic bliss and forget for a time the necessity of going to sea under such conditions for a living.

One long voyage I made after that, and only one, before finally settling down ashore. But the space allotted to me is gone, and even if I were to recapitulate the details of that voyage, I fear that in its likeness to the last one it would be somewhat monotonous. Again I found no trace of Christianity aboard. Again I found myself in a minority of one ; and so, although taking my friendless position into consideration I had naught to complain of on the ground of treatment, I was by no means sorry when at the end of the voyage I found it possible to quit the sea life altogether.

And if it should be thought that I have drawn too gloomy a picture, and that the title of this book should rightly have been ' *Without* Christ at Sea,' I can only humbly reply that the incidents which I have recorded are none of my choosing. I have tried with all my soul to say without bias what I remember of those days, in the mellowing light of memory, and my earnest hope and prayer is that some good may result.

Spottiswoode & Co. Printers, New-street Square, London.

www.ingramcontent.com/pod-product-compliance
Lightning Source LLC
Chambersburg PA
CBHW062035090426

42740CB00016B/2918